CRITICAL THINKING

READING, THINKING, AND REASONING SKILLS

S0-BXX-599

AUTHORS

Don Barnes
Professor of Education
Ball State University; Muncie, Indiana

Arlene Burgdorf
Former Resource Consultant
Hammond Indiana Public Schools

L. Stanley Wenck
Professor of Educational Psychology
Ball State University; Muncie, Indiana

CONSULTANT

Gloria Sesso
Supervisor of Social Studies
Half Hollow Hills School District; Dix Hills, New York

STECK-VAUGHN COMPANY

AUSTIN, TEXAS
A Division of National Education Corporation

Contributing Writers: Tara McCarthy and Linda Ward Beech

Text:

Every effort has been made to trace the ownership of all copyrighted material and to secure the necessary permissions to reprint these selections. In the event of any question arising as to the use of any material, the editor and publisher, while expressing regret for any inadvertent error, will be happy to make the necessary correction in future printings.

"An old silent pond" from CRICKET SONGS, Japanese haiku translated by Harry Behn. Copyright © 1964 by Harry Behn. All rights reserved. Reprinted by permission of Marian Reiner.

"The Bird of the Night" reprinted by permission of Macmillan Publishing Company from THE BAT-POET by Randall Jarrell. Copyright © Macmillan Publishing Company 1963, 1964.

Specified excerpt on page 13 of Chapter III in CHARLOTTE'S WEB by E. B. White. Copyright © 1952, by E. B. White. Renewed 1980 by E. B. White. Reprinted by permission of Harper & Row, Publishers, Inc.

Paragraphs reprinted by permission of Coward, McCann & Geogheghan from THE CORAL REEF by Gilda Berger, text copyright © 1977 by Gilda Berger.

Riddle and excerpt from THE HOBBIT by J. R. R. Tolkien. Copyright © 1977 by J. R. R. Tolkien. Reprinted by permission of Houghton Mifflin Company.

"Message from a Caterpillar" from LITTLE RACCOON AND POEMS FROM THE WOODS by Lilian Moore. Text copyright © by Lilian Moore. All rights reserved. Reprinted by permission of Marian Reiner for the author.

Excerpt from A NATURAL HISTORY OF NEW YORK CITY by John Francis Kiernan. Copyright © 1959 by John Francis Kiernan. Reprinted by permission of Houghton Mifflin Company.

Pictures to Read from PICK A PECK OF PUZZLES by Arnold Roth. Copyright © 1966 by Scholastic Book Services. Reprinted by permission of the author.

Excerpt from "The Runaway" from THE POETRY OF ROBERT FROST edited by Edward Connery Lathem. Copyright 1923, © 1969 by Henry Holt and Company. Copyright 1951 by Robert Frost. Reprinted by permission of Henry Holt and Company.

Codes adapted with permission of Macmillan Publishing Company from SECRET CODES AND CIPHERS by Joel Rothman and Ruthven Tremain. Copyright © by Joel Rothman and Ruthven Tremain.

Photography:

Cover – Bill Craft
p. 5 – Tom Athey
pp. 6, 39 – Bob Daemmrich/TexaStock
p. 17 – Krantzen Studio Inc.
p. 18 top left – Stephen Dalton/Animals Animals
p. 18 top right – Runk/Schoenberger/Grant Heilman
p. 18 bottom left – Runk/Schoenberger/Grant Heilman
p. 18 bottom right – Grant Heilman Photography
p. 20 – George McCaul
p. 21 – NASA
p. 40 left – Alvis Upitis/The Image Bank
p. 40 right – Gregory Heisler/The Image Bank
pp. 41, 105 – AP/Wide World Photos
p. 59 – Brad Doherty
p. 79 – David Brownell/The Image Bank
p. 82 – The Metropolitan Museum of Art
p. 89, 96 – The Granger Collection
p. 101 – Harvy R. Phillips/PPI
p. 119 – Terry Tullos Wayland
p. 127 – Photoworld/FPG
p. 128 – Phyllis Liedeker

Illustrations:

pp. 8, 12, 19, 22, 27, 43, 48, 49, 56, 68, 78, 118, 124 – Scott Bieser
pp. 26, 31, 36, 72, 92, 109 – Charles Varner/Carol Bancroft & Friends
pp. 28, 54, 55, 90, 99, 113, 114 – Keith Wilson
pp. 87, 103, 104 – Lynn McClain

ISBN 0-8114-1854-5
Copyright © 1987 by Steck-Vaughn Company, Austin, Texas
All rights reserved. No part of this book may be reproduced in any form or by any means, electronic or mechanical, including photocopying, recording, or by any information storage and retrieval system, without the written permission of the publisher. Printed and bound in the United States of America.

5 6 7 8 9 0 WC 90 89

KNOWING

Knowing means getting the facts together. Let's try it out. Look at the picture. Do you think these people have been traveling for a long time? What facts in the picture make you think that? Why have the people stopped? Do you think they should keep going or look for a place to spend the night? Why?

When you **classify**, you arrange things in groups according to some system. Read the following article, which tells about three major groups of musical instruments.

What is your favorite musical group? Whichever one it is, the musicians probably produce their wonderful sound by using three different kinds of instruments—wind, percussion, and stringed.

A percussion instrument, such as a drum, is played by striking it. A wind instrument, such as a horn, is played with the breath. A violin is an example of a stringed instrument—an instrument that produces sound through the plucking of its strings or through the movement of a bow across them.

Each item below is an example of one of the three kinds of instruments. Write **percussion**, **wind**, or **stringed** on the line after each word.

1. guitar _Stringed_
2. cymbals _percussion_
3. piccolo _wind_
4. cello _stringed_
5. triangles _percussion_

6. viola _stringed_
7. tuba _wind_
8. castanets _____
9. marimba _____
10. zither _____

There is a musical instrument that is both stringed **and** percussion. The musician strikes the keys. The keys, in turn, strike little hammers which cause strings to vibrate. Which musical instrument is this?

piano

Name _____

Critical Thinking, Gray Level. © 1987 Steck-Vaughn Co.

Often, items can be classified in more than one group. Each state listed below is either northeastern, southeastern, northwestern, or southwestern. Each state is also either small or large, and either coastal or inland. Write each state name under three correct headings. You may use a map of the United States to help you.

Alabama, Connecticut, Georgia, Oregon,
New Mexico, New York, Washington, Montana,
Rhode Island, South Carolina, Texas, Arizona

Northeastern	Southeastern	Northwestern	Southwestern

(more than 50,000 sq. mi.)	(less than 50,000 sq. mi.)		
Large	**Small**	**Coastal**	**Inland**

Name

Words and sentences can be classified as either **specific** or **general**. The ladders below show how words and sentences can be arranged. The top step on each ladder describes a general object or idea. The words and sentences become more specific as you move down the steps of the ladder.

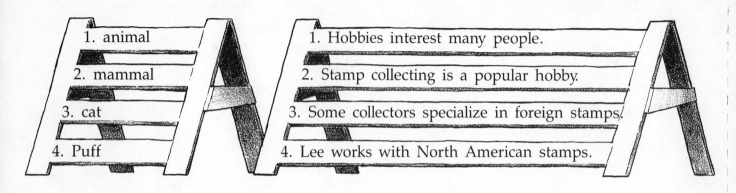

1. animal
2. mammal
3. cat
4. Puff

1. Hobbies interest many people.
2. Stamp collecting is a popular hobby.
3. Some collectors specialize in foreign stamps.
4. Lee works with North American stamps.

For each group below, number the items from **1** to **4**. Use **1** for the most general object or idea. The most specific object or idea will be number **4**.

1. encyclopedia _4_

   printed material _1_

   book _2_

   reference book _3_

2. boys _3_

   Charles _4_

   children _2_

   everyone _1_

3. TV _2_

   The Bong Show _4_

   entertainment _1_

   comedy show _3_

4. Kiwi _4_

   bird _2_

   parrot _3_

   pet _1_

5. shoes _3_

   clothing _1_

   sneakers _4_

   footwear _2_

6. jet _4_

   aircraft _2_

   vehicle _1_

   airplane _3_

7. A team sport attracts large crowds. _____

   The Lee High Lions pull a capacity crowd. _____

   People enjoy watching an athletic event. _____

   A football game is a crowded affair. _____

Name

Critical Thinking, Gray Level. © 1987 Steck-Vaughn Co.

You already know what a statement of **fact** is. A **fanciful** statement does more than state a fact. It creates a picture in your mind.

Example: Fact The rain fell heavily on the roof.
Fanciful The rain beat like a thousand thundering hoofbeats over my head.

A. Below are three fanciful statements based on everyday events. Change each statement so that it simply tells a fact.

1. Raquel was in such a rush that she just flew to school.

_____

2. Al's car is a chariot.

_____

3. Her brother acted like a monster.

_____

B. Change the statements of fact below into fanciful statements.

1. The calico kitten is especially brave.

_____

2. We won the game by several points.

_____

3. My shortwave radio can pick up many foreign stations.

_____

C. Write a fanciful paragraph about one of the following: autumn leaves, an airplane, a bird.

_____

_____

_____

_____

Name _____

People sometimes exaggerate to express strong feelings. For example, a person who says, "My mouth was on fire when I tasted that food," is reacting strongly to an unpleasant event. A simple statement of fact would be, "The taste of the strong, spicy food caused a burning sensation in my mouth."

Finish each sentence below by underlining the word or words in parentheses that will make the sentence a simple statement of fact.

1. There were (millions of, several, thousands of) mice scurrying around the old house.

2. When the branches of the old tree swayed, they (made a swishing sound, moaned and groaned, scared me to death).

3. The lights over the pond, which were probably caused by (UFO's, prowlers with flashlights, fireflies), gave me an eerie feeling as they twinkled off and on.

4. The winning wrestler, a huge man, was about (five feet, ten feet, six and one-half feet) tall.

5. The room is so cold that the temperature in here must be (zero, cold enough to freeze us to death, near freezing).

6. We saw a waterfall in the river that was (sky high, a hundred feet high, a mile high).

7. The new town hall will be (very beautiful, the finest in the land, the most impressive building in history).

8. The noise from the engine was loud enough to (split our eardrums, drive us crazy, almost deafen us for the moment).

9. My younger brother has grown (very rapidly, like a weed, by leaps and bounds).

10. She fell asleep in the noonday sun and woke up (with a sunburn, looking like a lobster, red as a beet).

Name

Critical Thinking, Gray Level. © 1987 Steck-Vaughn Co.

A **fact** is a statement that you can prove through evidence.

An **opinion** is a statement that represents your belief or judgment, but which you cannot yet prove.

A. Each sentence below contains a fact and an opinion. Put one line under the fact and two lines under the opinion.

1. John bought a new car which he thinks is the best car ever made.

2. Because she felt that she might get a lot of attention, Peg joined the basketball team.

3. Darren and Hank bravely walked into the forest which everyone believed was haunted.

4. "You surely have the most beautiful house in town," Lila said when she came to visit Judy.

5. When the class judged the pictures, most of the students thought Art's drawing was the best.

6. The grocery store has several new clerks who the manager thinks will do very well.

B. Write **F** before each fact and **O** before each opinion.

_____ 1. Most airplane crashes seem to be the fault of careless traffic controllers.

_____ 2. The process of filling a rubber tire with compressed air was invented in 1888.

_____ 3. Several countries claim ownership of land near the South Pole.

_____ 4. We have the greatest baseball team ever!

_____ 5. I think that plants have emotions and feelings.

Name _____

One week last summer, Lisa and Mimi visited their friend Meredith, who lives on a ranch. After the girls returned to their home in the city, they told their parents about the trip. Read the girls' statements below. Write **Fact** before each statement of fact. Write **Opinion** before each opinion.

_____ 1. "The ranch house was red brick with white trim," said Lisa.

_____ 2. "We watched the cowhands brand some calves," Mimi recalled.

_____ 3. "It seems to me that Meredith's family needs more help around the ranch," stated Lisa.

_____ 4. "I think ranch food is much better than the food we eat at home," announced Mimi.

_____ 5. "Meredith's family took us to see a rodeo," said Lisa.

_____ 6. "A rodeo is the most exciting sport in the world to watch!" exclaimed Mimi.

_____ 7. "That was the best vacation I'll ever have for the rest of my life!" announced Lisa.

_____ 8. "I'm definitely going to work on a ranch when I grow up," said Mimi.

_____ 9. "I have a feeling that Meredith's family will invite us back again sometime," said Lisa.

_____ 10. "I've already written and thanked them for showing us such a fine time," said Mimi.

Name

Critical Thinking, Gray Level. © 1987 Steck-Vaughn Co.

A. A **definition** of a word tells the meaning of that word. An **example** gives an illustration of a word. For each word below, choose the best definition and place its letter on the top line. Place the letter of the examples on the bottom line. The first one is done for you.

1. animal   _____I_____

            _____C_____

2. president   _____

            _____

3. building   _____

            _____

4. river   _____

            _____

5. spice   _____

            _____

A pepper, cloves, ginger, nutmeg

B a structure with four walls, a roof, and a floor

C cows, sheep, and oxen

D a large stream of water

E school, store, home

F Amazon, Mississippi, Nile

G Washington, Lincoln, Truman, Reagan

H a flavored or scented plant substance

I any living organism that is not a plant

J the head of our country

B. Find the definition of each of these words in a dictionary. Write the definition on the line after **definition**. If the dictionary gives examples, write them on the line after **examples**.

1. **container**   definition: _____

                 examples: _____

2. **fern**   definition: _____

                 examples: _____

3. **cat**   definition: _____

                 examples: _____

Name _____

A **definition** is the meaning of a word. An **example** is the name of an item that illustrates the word. For each missing word below, a definition and some examples are given. Write **D** before each definition and **E** before each group of examples. Then, unscramble the letters printed in color to find the word being defined. Write that word on the line at the right. The first one is done for you.

1. __D__ outerwear made of cloth

   __E__ hat   coat   gloves   clothes _____

2. _____ something to sit on

   _____ chair   bench   stool   _____

3. _____ vine   tree   tulip   grass   _____

   _____ a living thing that is not an animal

4. _____ something that covers or protects

   _____ house   tent   shed   lean-to   roof   _____

5. _____ any of a group of warm-blooded vertebrates with wings

   _____ wren   robin   starling   duck   _____

6. _____ any implement used to do work

   _____ hoe   pliers   hatchet   shovel   _____

7. _____ the condition of the atmosphere

   _____ wet   windy   calm   stormy   hot   breezy   _____

8. _____ nervous   joyful   tense   moody   giddy   _____

   _____ a strong feeling

Name _____

Critical Thinking, Gray Level. © 1987 Steck-Vaughn Co.

A **summary** is a statement that briefly gives the main idea of a longer selection.

A. Read the paragraph and the three summaries that follow it. Underline the summary that best explains the main idea of the article. Then explain why you chose that particular summary.

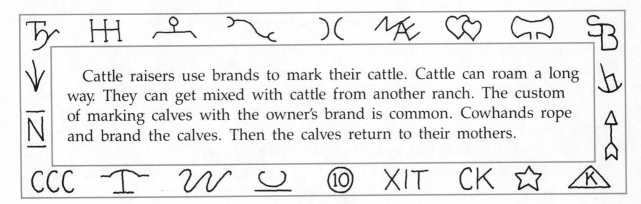

Cattle raisers use brands to mark their cattle. Cattle can roam a long way. They can get mixed with cattle from another ranch. The custom of marking calves with the owner's brand is common. Cowhands rope and brand the calves. Then the calves return to their mothers.

Summary 1. Branding cattle is not a very kind way to treat animals.

Summary 2. Ranchers brand cattle so that they will not lose the animals.

Summary 3. Many kinds of brands are used by ranchers. These brands help to find lost calves.

_____

_____

_____

B. Read the paragraph below. Then write a summary of it.

Cellulose is the woody part of plants that gives them stiffness. Without cellulose, people would be without thousands of articles they use every day. Cotton fibers, linen cloth, coco matting, and manila rope are largely cellulose. Wood, too, is mostly cellulose, as is the paper that is made from wood. Cellulose is also used in the manufacture of certain plastics.

_____

_____

_____

Name _____

An **outline** helps you organize and remember the main idea and the details that support the main idea.

A. Read the two paragraphs below. The main idea for each is given. Fill in the details that support each main idea.

The Confrontation

Detective Yoshi gasped in disbelief as he entered the room. Every drawer in the desk was overturned; the contents lay all over the floor. The lamps from each table were smashed, and the tables were upended. Each cushion on the couch was slashed; the insides had been yanked out. The closet door was off its hinges; and shirts, socks, and sweaters hung from the shelves and lay in heaps on the floor. Even the wastebaskets had been dumped and searched.

Detective Yoshi tiptoed to the window and peered out into the street below. There in the darkness, a limousine waited, its motor running. Inside, two burly men were talking quietly. A large box was between them. As the town clock sounded, the men leaned back and looked toward the window. The detective quietly stepped back.

I. A ransacked room

    A. _____

    B. _____

    C. _____

    D. _____

    E. _____

    F. _____

II. A waiting limousine

    A. _____

    B. _____

B. Plan an ending to the story. What would happen if the men and the detective had a confrontation? Use another sheet of paper to outline your thoughts.

Name

Critical Thinking, Gray Level. © 1987 Steck-Vaughn Co.

Use the facts in this article to fill in the outline below.

General reference maps give information about where things are located, which routes are available to travelers, and the distance from one point to another. One kind of general reference map is a road map. Road maps are used by car, bus, and truck drivers. Another kind is the charts used by ship captains and airplane pilots. A globe is also a general reference map. Its map is printed onto a ball to give a truer picture of the earth's surface. A book of general reference maps is called an atlas.

Special maps show one or more important details. A weather map showing rainfall is a special map. A physical map is a special map which shows the rise and fall of land and water. A political map is a special map which uses a different color for each country.

Main Kinds of Maps

I. General reference maps

    A. _____

    B. _____

    C. _____

    D. _____

II. Special maps

    A. _____

    B. _____

    C. _____

Name _____

Read the following article to find out about four kinds of animals. Then fill in the outline, telling what each animal **does** and what it **symbolizes**.

Animals and What They Symbolize

People have always enjoyed comparing animal activity to human behavior. As a result, animals have come to stand for certain things. The bee, for example, works continuously, producing honey and helping flowers grow. People, therefore, feel that the bee stands for hard work.

Spiders suck blood from the insects they trap in their webs. For this reason, spiders have become symbols of misers—people who become wealthy at the expense of others. Another animal, the snail, has come to symbolize laziness, because it moves so slowly.

The butterfly symbolizes the process of life itself. This is because butterflies go through four complete changes in their life cycle—from egg, to caterpillar, to chrysalis, to full-grown butterfly.

Outline

I. The bee

    A. _____

    B. _____

II. The spider

    A. _____

    B. _____

III. The snail

    A. _____

    B. _____

IV. The butterfly

    A. _____

    B. _____

Name _____

Critical Thinking, Gray Level. © 1987 Steck-Vaughn Co.

A. Definition and Example

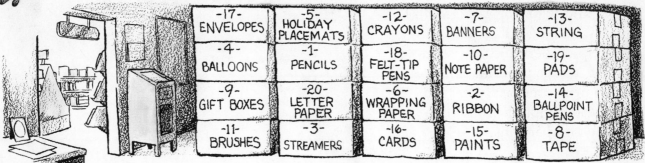

The picture above shows 20 boxes of supplies delivered to a small shop. After each definition below, write the numbers of the boxes that hold examples of the item defined. Some numbers may be placed after more than one definition.

1. **stationery**: material to be written on _____

2. **writing tools**: materials with which marks are made _____

3. **decorations**: materials used as ornaments _____

4. **packaging**: materials used to enclose, wrap, or bundle items _____

B. Outlining

Use your completed activity A above to make an outline of supplies delivered to the store.

_____

_____

_____

_____

_____

_____

_____

Name

C. Real and Fanciful

1. In the following paragraph, a writer described **dew**. To help readers picture the dew, the writer used fanciful comparisons. As you read the description, underline the comparisons.

   Little drops of dew sparkle like diamonds as they roll down the power lines like marbles. As the sun rises, the drops blink like traffic lights as they sway on the lines with the early morning breeze.

2. Study the photo of the raging waterfall. Use fanciful comparisons to write a paragraph that describes the waterfall.

_____

_____

_____

_____

_____

D. Fact and Opinion

1. Write a sentence that states a fact about the waterfall. _____

_____

2. Write a sentence that states your opinion about the waterfall. _____

_____

Name _____

Critical Thinking, Gray Level. © 1987 Steck-Vaughn Co.

UNDERSTANDING

Understanding means telling about something in your own words. Look at the picture. How is the person dressed? Do you know why? What kind of machine is shown in the picture? What is it used for? In your own words, explain what is happening in the picture. Tell how the person got there and what the person is doing.

To **compare** means to identify **likenesses**. To **contrast** means to identify **differences**.

Mallard Duck	Blue Jay

A. Study the birds shown in the picture.

   1. Compare the birds by listing two ways in which they are alike.

      a. _____

      b. _____

   2. Contrast the birds by listing two ways in which they are different.

      a. _____

      b. _____

B. Read the following paragraph. Then list two ways in which the hornbill and the mallee fowl are alike and two ways in which they are different.

   The African hornbill and the Australian mallee fowl have unusual nest-building habits. The mallee's nest is built of many layers, with each egg resting on a different layer. The hornbill's nest has hardened mud walls. Within these nests, the eggs incubate—the mallee eggs for about seven weeks, and the hornbill eggs for five.

   After the two kinds of chicks hatch, both must dig through barriers. The mallee chick must dig through the layers of the nest to the top. The hornbill chick must peck through the hard mud walls to escape.

Likenesses	Differences
1. _____	1. _____
2. _____	2. _____

Name _____

Critical Thinking, Gray Level. © 1987 Steck-Vaughn Co.

A. Each sentence group below **compares** two things, or shows how they are alike. On the line after each group, write a sentence which **contrasts** the things, or shows how they are different.

1. A chair and a bed are both furniture. They both have four legs. _____

_____

2. An auditorium is designed for recreation, as is a gymnasium. Both are large and

hold many people. _____

_____

3. Pins and needles are both used for sewing. They are small, sharp objects meant

to hold material together. _____

_____

4. Soccer and football are both team sports involving the use of a ball. Players

attempt to move the ball toward a goal. _____

_____

5. Diamonds and iron are both hard. Both must be brought out from mines.

_____

B. For each pair of items below, write a sentence to tell how the items are alike.

1. A tractor and a pair of roller skates _____

_____

2. A tree and an umbrella _____

_____

3. A diary and a telephone _____

_____

4. A guitar and a bird _____

_____

Name _____

Read the following description of a **hobbit**. Then, at the bottom of the page, write a paragraph in which you both compare and contrast yourself to one of these fanciful creatures.

I suppose hobbits need some description nowadays, since they have become rare and shy of the Big People, as they call us. They are (or were) a little people, about half our height, and smaller than the bearded Dwarves. Hobbits have no beards. There is little or no magic about them, except the ordinary everyday sort which helps them to disappear quietly and quickly when large stupid folk like you and me come blundering along, making a noise like elephants which they can hear a mile off. They are inclined to be fat in the stomach; they dress in bright colours (chiefly green and yellow); wear no shoes, because their feet grow natural leathery soles and thick warm brown hair like the stuff on their heads (which is curly); have long clever brown fingers, good-natured faces, and laugh deep fruity laughs (especially after dinner, which they have twice a day when they can get it).

— from *The Hobbit* by J.R.R. Tolkien

_____

_____

_____

_____

_____

_____

_____

_____

_____

_____

Name _____

Critical Thinking, Gray Level. © 1987 Steck-Vaughn Co.

A **cinquain** is a special kind of five-line poem. A cinquain may follow either of the forms, or structures, described on this page.

A. Study the cinquain at the bottom of the page. Decide which structure it follows. Then copy the cinquain on the five lines next to that structure.

B. On the remaining five lines, write your own cinquain, following the cinquain structure next to it.

Structure I

Line 1: one noun stating the subject _____

Line 2: two adjectives describing the noun _____

Line 3: three action verbs _____

Line 4: four words showing feeling about the subject _____

Line 5: another word for the word in Line 1 _____

Structure II

Line 1: two syllables naming the subject _____

Line 2: four syllables describing the subject _____

Line 3: six syllables showing action _____

Line 4: eight syllables showing feeling about the subject _____

Line 5: two syllables that stand for the word or words in Line 1 _____

My hat
Fuzzy, warm, soft
Protects, covers, cuddles
Makes a whirl of color on snow
Ski cap

Name _____

Letters make up the structure of a written word. In the word games below, you will play with the structure of words to form other words. In both games, you will be forming **synonyms**, or words that have almost the same meaning.

A. In each word pair below, take a letter from the top word and place it in the bottom word to make a pair of synonyms. Keep the letters of the bottom word in the same order. The first pair has been done for you.

1. leash _____lash_____   3. boast _____   5. turns _____

   bat _____beat_____   hip _____   pin _____

2. stalk _____   4. furry _____   6. quiet _____

   peak _____   age _____   lave _____

B. Change the order of the letters in both words of each pair below to form pairs of synonyms. The first pair has been done for you.

1. cork _____rock_____   4. heat _____   8. peels _____

   notes _____stone_____ tested _____   pan _____

2. strut _____   5. paws _____   9. fare _____

   lyre _____   tread _____   dared _____

3. stop _____   6. carve _____   10. least _____

   saint _____   reside _____   orb _____

                          7. leap _____

                          grin _____

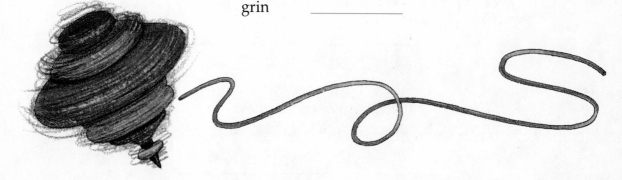

Name _____

Critical Thinking, Gray Level. © 1987 Steck-Vaughn Co.

A. The pictures below make a cartoon. They are similar to a filmstrip. On the lines below the pictures, write what you think is happening in each picture.

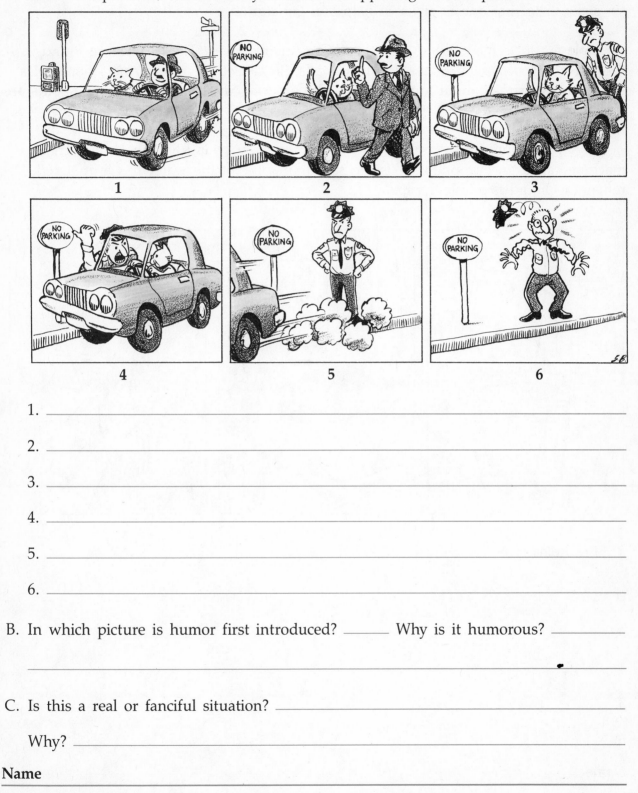

1. _____

2. _____

3. _____

4. _____

5. _____

6. _____

B. In which picture is humor first introduced? _____ Why is it humorous? _____

_____

C. Is this a real or fanciful situation? _____

Why? _____

Name _____

Read the paragraphs below to learn the steps used to make maple syrup. On the lines below the paragraphs, use your own words to tell the steps in order. There are six steps. The first one is given to help you get started.

Maple syrup is made from the sap of sugar maple trees. These trees are found in the northeastern United States and in Canada. To collect the sap, farmers bore holes into the tree trunks about four feet from the ground. Small metal or plastic spouts are forced into the holes. Buckets are hung from the spouts to collect sap as it flows from the holes.

The sap is poured into large tanks and is moved by sleds to a sap house. There a machine called an evaporator boils the sap until some of the water has evaporated. The remaining liquid is maple syrup.

1. Bore holes into tree trunks.

2. _____

3. _____

4. _____

5. _____

6. _____

Name

Critical Thinking, Gray Level. © 1987 Steck-Vaughn Co.

Figure and **figural** are words that refer to such things as charts, diagrams, and symbols. Such figures can help you see and understand quickly how facts are related.

A. Study the **bar graph** below. Then complete the sentences that follow it.

POINTS MADE IN A GAME

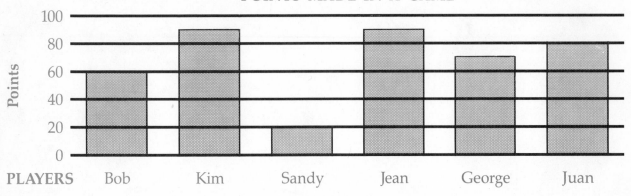

1. _____ and _____ tied for first place.

2. _____ came in second, with a score of _____.

3. _____ got 40 fewer points than _____ did.

B. The **line graph** below shows George's scores for six different games. Study the graph. Then complete the sentences and answer the question that follow it.

POINTS SCORED BY GEORGE

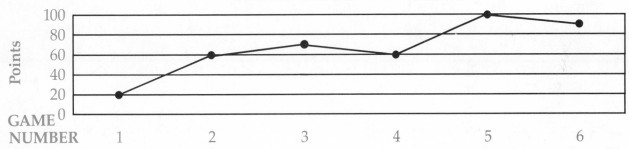

1. George got his highest score in _____.

2. The first time he played, George's score was _____.

3. George's scores were the same in games _____ and _____.

4. In general, did George improve, get worse, or stay about the same as he played

the game? _____

Name

The figures below—with their circles, letters, and colors—make up what is called a **three-circle code**. The **key** below the code shows the symbols that can be used for the letters in the first circle.

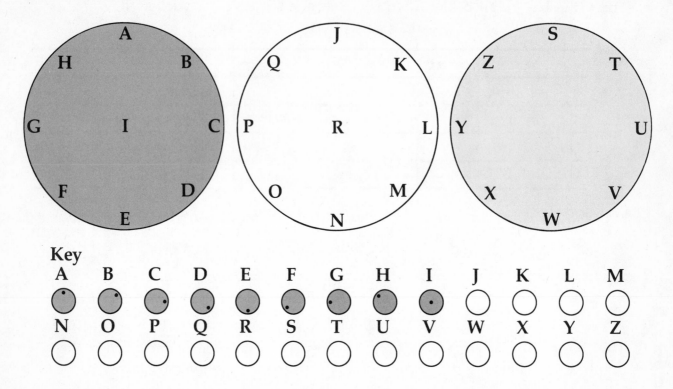

A. Complete the Key to show the symbols for the letters in the second and third circles. Use a pencil—lightly—to indicate the gray color used in the third circle.

B. Use a regular pencil and a colored pencil to encode the following saying: **It is better to be safe than sorry**.

C. Decode the following to find another saying.

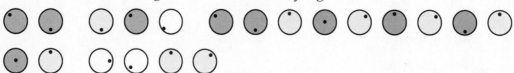

Name

Critical Thinking, Gray Level. © 1987 Steck-Vaughn Co.

Read the words in each group below. Then find the word in the **Word List** that is related to each word in the group and write it on the line. The first one is done for you.

<u>   pin   </u>   1. straight, safety, bowling, clothes, rolling

_____   2. pig, ball-point, bull, play

_____   3. wagon, steering, potter's, ship's, spinning

_____   4. circus, boxing, tree, bathtub, telephone

_____   5. sea, egg, pie, snail

_____   6. movie, general's, shooting, lucky

_____   7. false, gear, saw, rake, comb

_____   8. mystery, picture, short, news

_____   9. home, dinner, paper, license

_____   10. hospital, flower, water, rock

_____   11. spy, eye, field, drinking, window

_____   12. piano, musical, lock, answer, code

_____   13. multiplication, dining, time

_____   14. night, flash, sun, sky

_____   15. finger, toe, roofing, finishing, six-penny

Word List

wheel
story
key
shell
pen
ring
teeth
light
pin
plate
nail
glass
bed
star
table

Name

Below are two games of Word Tic-Tac-Toe. In each bracket, a word is printed above

the line: | ___huge___ . Pick a synonym for the word from the list below.

Write the synonym below the word: | ___huge___ / gigantic . The first player to complete

a row of brackets across, up and down, or diagonally is the winner. Not all of the words will be used.

SYNONYM SEARCH BOX

hug
qualified
elect
mislay
tumult
miniature
radiant
rapid
reaction
ready
genuine
violin
reap
revolt
restore
remember
still
sensational
foolish
show
tremble
vanish
surprise
vague
accentuate
expire
ragged

GAME I

emphasize	embrace	eligible
elapse	misplace	shining
choose	uproar	tattered

GAME II

swift	real	rebuild
response	harvest	recall
prepared	rebellion	thrilling

Critical Thinking, Gray Level. © 1987 Steck-Vaughn Co.

Name _____

A good paragraph is built around a **main idea**. Often, this main idea is stated in a **topic sentence**. At other times, there is no topic sentence, though the facts in the paragraph are still clustered around a main idea.

A. Read each paragraph below. If the paragraph has a topic sentence, underline that sentence.

 1.   Water has many unusual properties. For example, a skin forms where water meets air. Tiny water droplets squeeze together and move upward through stems and leaves. Water also floats when it is frozen, because frozen water has expanded and become less dense.

 2.   One hero of the First World War was a pigeon that carried an important message through artillery fire. During the Second World War, the British dropped boxes of homing pigeons behind enemy lines. Pigeons were also used to carry messages during the Korean War.

 3.   The camel is well-equipped for desert travel. Its long eyelashes help keep the blowing sand out of its eyes. A camel can travel for several days without water. Thick pads protect its hoofs from the hot sand.

 4.   A hippopotamus can run on the bottom of a lake or river at eight miles an hour. On land, it can run as fast as a human. This large animal is a fast swimmer and can dive, sink like a rock, or float like a log.

 5.   Though insects are small, many of them can cause great damage. Some insects can destroy crops. Others can cause various illnesses in people and in other animals.

B. A good title states the main idea briefly and in an interesting way. On the following lines, write a title for each paragraph above.

 1. _____

 2. _____

 3. _____

 4. _____

 5. _____

Name _____

Read each group of sentences below. Decide which sentence seems unrelated to the others, and draw a line through it. Then think of a **main-idea**, or **topic**, sentence that could be used to introduce the remaining three sentences. Write a paragraph, using your topic sentence and following it with the three related sentences.

A. 1. Native Americans could tell direction in the forest by examining where moss grew.
   2. Broken branches and twigs were clues to the paths taken by forest animals.
   3. Native Americans told a variety of myths and legends.
   4. Keen ears could pick up the special sounds made by different birds and mammals.

_____

_____

_____

_____

_____

B. 1. The investigations of scientists have led to the cures for many diseases.
   2. Scientists hold conventions frequently.
   3. A scientist's patient investigations can also unfold important facts about the earth and about the universe.
   4. The results of any investigation lead to new and fascinating questions which may be answered by further study.

_____

_____

_____

_____

_____

Name _____

Critical Thinking, Gray Level. © 1987 Steck-Vaughn Co.

Events are often related in **time**. Often, words such as **then**, **next**, or **as** are clues that let you know the time order that relates the events.

Read the sentences below and follow these three steps.

A. Circle the clue word or phrase that shows the time relationship between the events.

B. If one event happened before the other, underline the part of the sentence that tells what happened first.

C. If both events happened at the same time, put a check on the line before the sentence.

_____ 1. When Jim drove the car into the driveway, he noticed that the garage door was open.

_____ 2. He carefully eased out from under the wheel, after parking the car.

_____ 3. Before he even opened the door to the house, Jim could tell that something strange was going on.

_____ 4. As Jim entered the kitchen, he heard odd noises coming from the living room.

_____ 5. He was not frightened until the noises got louder.

_____ 6. He hesitated, and then walked bravely through the kitchen to the hall.

_____ 7. Outside the living room, Jim's heart pounded while the strange noises continued.

_____ 8. After deciding to look now or never, Jim yanked the door open.

_____ 9. When he looked around, Jim was surprised to see only his father with some friends.

_____ 10. Looking puzzled, Jim stepped into the room and then smiled with relief.

_____ 11. At the same moment, Jim's father turned on some new electronic drum machines.

_____ 12. After Jim's excitement was over, his father showed him how to use the drum machines.

Name

Events are often related because one event causes the other to happen. This is called a **cause-effect** relationship. Clue words such as **because**, **since**, and **as a result** often signal a cause-effect relationship.

A. Read the following paragraphs. In each blank, write a clue word or phrase which points out the cause-effect relationship between the events.

   1. Before the invention of the steam engine, ships used the power of the wind to move across the seas. It took from three to four weeks to sail from America to

      Europe. _____ the winds generally blew from west to east, it took longer to go from Europe to America.

   2. During the last century, pioneers began to have a difficult time finding vast

      stretches of land in the East. _____, they started to travel westward across the country in covered wagons.

   3. Seashell collecting was once a popular

      hobby. _____ many
      varieties of seashells have now become
      rare, ecologists are discouraging people
      from continuing this hobby.

B. Complete each sentence to make it show a cause-effect relationship.

   1. The team won the tournament because _____

      _____

   2. Our field trip was a success because _____

      _____

   3. Since it is beginning to snow, our trip to the mountains _____

      _____

   4. New speed-limit laws were passed, and, as a result, _____

      _____

Name _____

Critical Thinking, Gray Level. © 1987 Steck-Vaughn Co.

The first two sentences in each group below tell about events that at first do not seem to be related to one another. The third sentence, however, tells about an event that was caused by the first two. On the lines below each word group, explain the cause-effect relationship.

1. Mrs. Brown bought a toy in New York. Six-year-old Vivian lived in Seattle. Vivian played with her new toy. _____

   _____

   _____

2. Mountains near the town of Troy received heavy rainfall. In the valley some miles away was a small stream. Rather suddenly the small stream flooded. _____

   _____

   _____

3. Mr. and Mrs. Roberts were robbed one dark night. Jane Roberts was away at college, studying accounting. Jane began to look for a job. _____

   _____

   _____

4. The price of gasoline rose a great deal. Yuji works in a city several miles from his home. Yuji now rides to work with three other people. _____

   _____

   _____

5. Several stores suddenly closed. The power company moved to another town. The school enrollment dropped. _____

   _____

   _____

Name _____

Sometimes objects or ideas are related according to how they are arranged in a space. Such relationships are called **spatial relationships**. To understand a spatial relationship, you must move your eyes not only from left to right, as you do in reading, but also up and down and all around.

Study the drawings below. Then answer the questions and do the activities that follow them.

_____ _____ _____ _____

A. Write two sentences to tell two ways in which all the drawings are alike.

   1. _____

   2. _____

   _____

B. On the line below each drawing, spell out the word shown in the drawing.

C. Now use what you have learned about spatial relationships to make drawings of the following words:

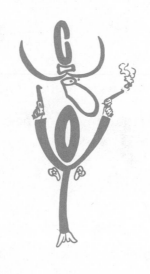 

_____ _____

1. escalator	2. whale	3. chain	4. (your own name)

Name

Critical Thinking, Gray Level. © 1987 Steck-Vaughn Co.

This photograph was taken after a marathon race. As you study the picture, imagine that you are the newspaper reporter who will write about the race.

A. Identifying Main Ideas

Write a headline to accompany the photo. Your headline should state the main idea.

_____

B. Comparing and Contrasting

On the lines below, make notes comparing and contrasting the runners shown in the photograph.

How the Runners Are Alike   **How the Runners Are Different**

_____   _____

_____   _____

C. Identifying Relationships

Write a caption to go with the photo. Make up names for the winner and the runners-up. Your caption should show **time relationships** with the words **first**, **next**, and **last**. You might also include a **cause-effect relationship** to explain how the winner won the race.

_____

_____

_____

_____

Name _____

39

Refer to the photographs as you complete the following activities.

D. Figural Relationships

The football player and the dancer are in similar positions. Tell as specifically as possible how their positions are alike.

_____

_____

E. Comparing and Contrasting

How are their activities different?

_____

_____

F. Steps in a Process

Imagine that you are either a dancer preparing for a performance or a football player preparing to play in a Bowl game. List the steps you must take to make sure that you do well in the performance or the game.

_____

_____

_____

_____

Name
_____

Critical Thinking, Gray Level. © 1987 Steck-Vaughn Co.

APPLYING

Applying means using what you know. Look at the picture. What are the men doing? How can you tell that they are members of the same community? What do you think the men will do after they finish the roof? How long do you think it will take the men to finish building the barn?

Objects can be put in different **orders**, according to the standard you are using. In the activities below, you will use two different standards for ordering objects.

A. Number the words in each column from **1** to **6** according to the number of syllables each word contains.

1	2	3
_____ information	_____ restriction	_____ cottonwood
_____ outward	_____ electronically	_____ automatically
_____ source	_____ ocean	_____ cough
_____ mathematically	_____ invisibly	_____ fiddle
_____ photograph	_____ fair	_____ grammatical
_____ organization	_____ superintendent	_____ metropolitan

B. Arrange the figures below in order according to the size of the shaded parts. Write **1** on the line below the figure with smallest shaded part and continue numbering until the largest part is numbered **8**.

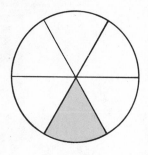 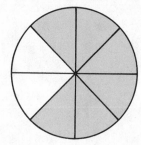 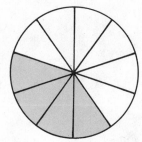 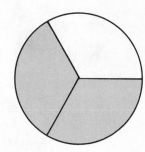

_____   _____   _____   _____

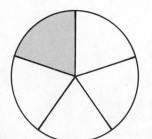 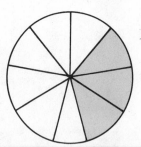 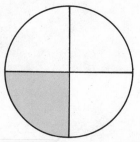 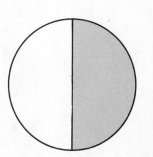

_____   _____   _____   _____

Name

Critical Thinking, Gray Level. © 1987 Steck-Vaughn Co.

A. Number each column of objects from the thinnest to the thickest. Write **1** before the thinnest. Continue until the thickest is labeled **3**. The first column is done for you.

1	**2**	**3**
__2__ pamphlet	_____ rope	_____ branch
__3__ book	_____ string	_____ trunk
__1__ paper	_____ thread	_____ twig

B. In the groups below, order the objects according to weight. Use **1** for the lightest, **3** for the heaviest, and **2** for the object that is in between.

_____ dog	_____ quart	_____ ton
_____ mouse	_____ pint	_____ ounce
_____ elephant	_____ gallon	_____ pound

C. Think of two different standards you could use to order the objects at the bottom of the page. Then write the different standards on the column-heading lines and list the objects.

Standard 1: _____   Standard 2: _____

_____   _____

_____   _____

_____   _____

Name _____

A. List the products below according to their importance to human life, their cost, and their durability (how long they last).

television, bread, car, bed, house, piano, light bulb

1	2	3
Most important first	Most expensive first	Longest lasting first

B. List some animals that are useful to humans and explain the uses. When your list is complete, number from the most useful animal to the least.

Animal	Uses

Name

Critical Thinking, Gray Level. © 1987 Steck-Vaughn Co.

An **estimate** is a rough judgment about how long or large something is or about how long it will take to accomplish a task. While an estimate is not exact, it is somewhat more reliable than a **guess**. That is because an estimate is based on some kind of standard, such as a picture, a scale, a key, or your own experience.

Study the map and the key. Then on the chart below the map, write your estimates of the distance between the various cities shown on the map. An estimate of the distance between Miami and Seattle has already been given to help you get started.

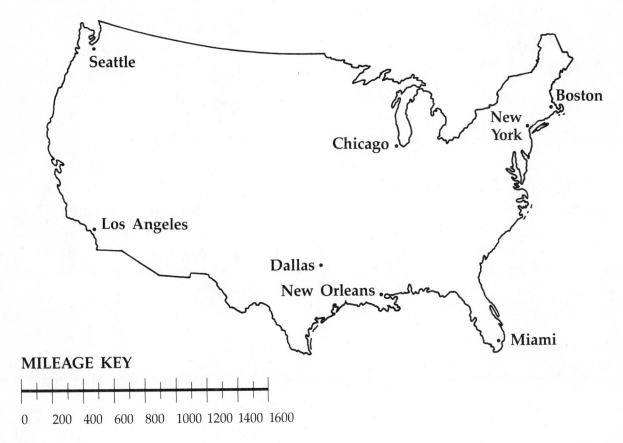

MILEAGE KEY

0   200 400 600 800 1000 1200 1400 1600

	Boston	New Orleans	Chicago	Seattle
New York				
Miami				3200
Los Angeles				
Dallas				

Name

A. Estimate the amount of time it would take **you**—working at the top of your form—to do each of the following chores:

1. paint a 6-foot-by-4-foot bookcase _____

2. wash breakfast dishes for a family of four _____

3. buy a three-day supply of groceries _____

4. read 20 pages in a history book _____

5. clean out a small aquarium _____

6. write a composition about autumn _____

7. clean out your desk _____

B. Now imagine that you have been asked to do all the tasks listed above in a single day. On the chart below, make a schedule. In the right-hand column, list the chores in the order in which you would prefer to do them. In the column at the left, show as closely as possible—in hours and minutes—when you would begin the task and when you would probably finish it. For example, you might write 8 A.M. — 8:30 A.M. to show the time span for doing a chore.

TIME	CHORE

Name

Critical Thinking, Gray Level. © 1987 Steck-Vaughn Co.

A **probability** is something that is very likely to happen. For example, if you do not water a plant for a long time, it is **probable** that the plant will die.

A. Complete each sentence below by telling what the **probable** outcome will be.

1. If it does not rain for some time, it is probable that _____

_____

2. If the school band practices hard every day, it is probable that the band concert

_____

3. If a player throws a ball at the basketball hoop 100 times, it is probable that

_____

4. If you forget to bring your lunch to school, it is probable that _____

_____

5. If you manage to save one dollar every week, it is probable that you will be able

to _____

B. A situation may have more than one probable outcome. Read about the situations below. Then list two probable outcomes for each situation.

1. Mary and Ian are scheduled to play a piano duet on Friday. They are both excellent players, but they have practiced very little together. Mary and Ian will probably

   a. _____

   b. _____

2. Leon is very shy. He has worked very hard to learn Spanish. As a result, he has been offered a chance to live with a family in Latin America this summer, along with students from other schools who have done well in Spanish. Leon will probably

   a. _____

   b. _____

Name _____

You know that a **probability** is something that is very likely to happen. A **possibility**, on the other hand, is something that **might** or **could** happen if certain other conditions happened, too.

A. Read each sentence below. Then write **probability** or **possibility** on the line before the sentence.

1. _____ This week, someone in your class will get a score of 90 or above on a paper or test.

2. _____ This winter, areas of the Northeast will get heavy snowfalls and high winds.

3. _____ This year, a severe earthquake will hit the area in which you live.

4. _____ Within the next ten years, intelligent beings from another galaxy will visit Earth.

5. _____ Within the next ten years, all the nations of the Western Hemisphere will unite to form one nation.

B. Select two of the sentences in part A which you have labeled **possible**. On the lines below, tell what you would **probably** do or how your life would **probably** change, if such an event actually happened.

1. _____

_____

_____

_____

2. _____

_____

_____

_____

Critical Thinking, Gray Level. © 1987 Steck-Vaughn Co.

Name

To **infer** means to reach a conclusion based on what you observe or the facts you have at hand.

Study the picture of the house. Examine the details carefully. Then write a paragraph to tell what you **infer** about the house. For example, do you infer that the house is empty or occupied? Do you infer that people in the neighborhood like or dislike this particular house? For each inference that you make, give at least one picture-detail that has led you to that inference.

_____

_____

_____

_____

_____

_____

Name

Many times, an inference is correct. You have enough facts at hand to lead you logically to the correct conclusion. At other times, however, an inference may **not** be correct. As you gather additional information, your inference may change. You may come to a different conclusion.

Here are some facts that may lead you to change your inference about the house you studied on page 49:

- The owner, Mr. M., is old and ill.
- Mr. M.'s wife and other close relatives died sometime ago.
- Mr. M. is extremely shy.
- Mr. M. has very little money.

1. On the basis of the facts above, write a few sentences which explain the condition of the house shown in the picture on page 49.

_____

_____

_____

_____

2. On the basis of the facts above, what would you infer about the kinds of things that Mr. M. needs most?

_____

_____

_____

3. In many cases, it is important to check further to make sure an inference is correct. How would you check to see whether the inference you made in number 2 is correct?

_____

_____

_____

Critical Thinking, Gray Level. © 1987 Steck-Vaughn Co.

Read each paragraph. Then read the sentences below it. If you can **infer** the correct ending for the sentence from the facts given in the paragraph, underline that ending. On the line below the sentence, copy the key word or words from the paragraph that led you to that inference.

If you **cannot** infer the answer from the facts in the paragraph, do not underline any of the sentence endings.

A.   Janet slowly opened the door, got in, and sat down. Then she gradually pulled away from the curb. She waved good-bye and started out on her long journey.

  1. Janet is getting into a (plane, house, car).

  _____

  2. She is going (to the store, on a trip, to school).

  _____

  3. She will not return for several (weeks, days, months).

  _____

  4. Her mood is (happy, nervous, solemn).

  _____

B.   The wind gently waved the new grass on the empty prairie. The sky was cloudless. The moon had just come up.

  1. It is (morning, afternoon, evening). _____

  2. The weather is (clear, threatening, cold). _____

  3. The land is (flat, mountainous, forested). _____

C.   The fiery disc seemed white-hot overhead. The land was dry and barren. There seemed to be no hope of a rain cloud ever covering that fiery disc.

  1. The disc is (the moon, a floodlight, the sun). _____

  2. The land is (mountainous, desert, woodland). _____

  3. There are (no, few, many) houses in the area. _____

Name _____

Read the following paragraphs. Then write answers to the questions.

Most of us have witnessed the spectacular sight of the full moon rising over the horizon. How huge the moon seems at that time! Yet hours later, when the full moon is high in the sky above us, it seems to have become very much smaller — almost as if a silver dollar had become a dime. Indeed, many people do infer that the full moon has somehow diminished in size in its ride across the night sky.

Scientists have taken photographs of the full moon at both its rising stage and its late-night stage. When the diameter of the moon is measured in these photographs, it is exactly the same! The big-moon/little-moon experience that we have is thus an optical illusion—a trick played on our eyes.

An ancient Greek scientist, Ptolemy, supposed that the moon on the horizon looks larger to us because we are comparing it with trees, buildings, and other objects along the horizon-line. Yet, on the open sea—where there are no smaller objects with which to compare the rising moon—the same optical illusion takes place. Much more recently, scientists are guessing that the moon looks smaller when it is high in the sky because most objects tend to look smaller when we view them with raised eyes.

1. What have most people inferred about the size of the rising moon as compared with the same moon later in the night?

   _____

   _____

2. What are the facts concerning the full moon at different times of the night?

   _____

   _____

3. Why is Ptolemy's inference about the rising moon incorrect?

   _____

   _____

4. Today, what are scientists inferring about the reason for the optical illusion of big-moon/little-moon?

   _____

   _____

Name _____

Critical Thinking, Gray Level. © 1987 Steck-Vaughn Co.

We often understand the meaning of a word only when we hear or read it in **context**—that is, in connection with other words. This is true of even simple words, such as **trunk**. **Trunk** can mean **(1)** part of a tree, **(2)** part of an elephant, or **(3)** a large container in which to pack clothes or other belongings.

A. Above the word **trunk** in the sentence below, write the number of the meaning that applies to it.

The elephant picked up the trunk with his trunk and set it next to the trunk of the banyan tree.

B. Study each sentence and the underlined words in it. Then rewrite the sentence, replacing one of the underlined words with a word or phrase that has a similar meaning. You may use a dictionary.

1. He had the ill fortune of losing his fortune in the stock market.

_____

_____

2. She was not the type to type for long hours at a time.

_____

_____

3. At the peak of his career, the explorer went to the peak of Mt. Everest.

_____

_____

4. He was last seen wrapped in a cape and walking along the shore of the cape.

_____

_____

5. She will study this at home in her study.

_____

_____

Name

A. A simple word—such as *run*—often can be combined with other words to form a phrase that has a special meaning. Read each sentence below and the expressions that follow it. Then, in the blank, write the expression that most sensibly fits the context of the sentence.

1. It is always pleasant to ———————— a friend.
   a. run over   b. run out of   c. run into

2. The detective ———————— the man's alibi.
   a. saw through   b. saw off   c. saw out

3. Midway through the race, Leonard ————————.
   a. fell under   b. fell behind   c. fell off

4. The crowd ———————— in amazement as the magician performed.
   a. looked out   b. looked on   c. looked over

5. In her appearance, Susan ———————— her mother.
   a. takes after   b. takes over   c. takes to

B. In the first column below, copy the expressions you used in the sentences in part A. In the second column, write the meaning of that expression. You may use a dictionary.

   Expression   **Meaning**

   1. ————————————   ————————————————————

   2. ————————————   ————————————————————

   3. ————————————   ————————————————————

   4. ————————————   ————————————————————

   5. ————————————   ————————————————————

Name ————————————————————————————————

Critical Thinking, Gray Level. © 1987 Steck-Vaughn Co.

As time goes by our language changes. Many words take on new meanings and often leave their old meanings behind. In the **Word Box** are ten such words. Read the **old meanings** and the **new meanings** below. Then choose the word from the **Word Box** that is being defined or described and write it on the line.

Word Box

person	duck	slip	left	snob
dice	girl	villain	tinker	gossip

	Old Meaning	New Meaning
1. _____	a child of either sex	a young female
2. _____	a farm worker	a wicked person
3. _____	weak, worthless	one side of something
4. _____	to dive	to move one's head quickly
5. _____	slime	to slide suddenly
6. _____	a mender of pans	to work in a useless way
7. _____	a character in a play	an individual
8. _____	a shoemaker's helper	someone who snubs others
9. _____	to give	to cut food in small bits
10. _____	a godparent	to chat idly

Name _____

In Lewis Carroll's book *Through the Looking-Glass*, the main character—Alice—hears the following poem:

'Twas brillig, and the slithy toves

    Did gyre and gimble in the wabe:

All mimsy were the borogroves,

    And the mome raths outgrabe.

Here is what Alice said about the poem: "It seems very pretty, but it's **rather** hard to understand! Somehow it seems to fill my head with ideas—only I don't know exactly what they are!"

A. Begin to unravel the mystery of the nonsense poem.
   1. Draw **one** line under all the words you think are **nouns**.
   2. Draw **two** lines under all the words you think are **adjectives**, or describing words.
   3. **Circle** all the words you think are **action verbs**.

B. When you have completed part A correctly, you are ready to write your very own sensible version of the poem. Do this by filling in the blanks below with nouns, verbs, and adjectives of your own choosing.

'Twas _____, and the _____ _____

    Did _____ and _____ in the _____:

All _____ were the _____,

    And the _____ _____ _____.

C. Share your poem with your classmates. If the poem now makes sense, you have shown how well you know the English language and how skillfully you can work with it.

Critical Thinking, Gray Level. © 1987 Steck-Vaughn Co.

Name _____

Ordering Objects
Estimating

BACKDOOR

ENTRANCE

Mr. and Mrs. White have just bought a row of three stores. One is a stationery shop, one is a gift shop, and one is a hardware store. The Whites have combined the shops to make one large store which sells stationery, gifts, and hardware.

On the floor plan above, write labels to show how you would arrange and order the various items. Keep in mind that customers need to find the things they want easily and that the store must also look attractive and appealing.

Suppose that it is now October 1. The Whites have announced that the new store will open on October 12. On the lines list the tasks that must be carried out before the store can open.

Inferring

To buy and combine three stores is a big project. What inferences can you make about the Whites and the town they live in? Answers will vary. Possibilities:

Name

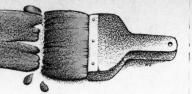

C. Anticipating Probabilities

On opening day, Mr. White gave copies of the following memo to all the employees. Read the memo. Then, on the lines below it, tell two **probable** feelings or reactions the employees would have.

MEMO

To all employees:

    It is imperative that all employees arrive at the store exactly one-half hour before its opening, which occurs at nine o'clock in the morning. Employees must be dressed suitably in freshly washed and pressed clothing. A list of official work assignments will be displayed on the framed bulletin board situated at the rear door of our establishment. Midday dining hours will be arranged for each employee after a conference concerning the necessity of keeping the store well-staffed throughout the shopping day. Employees may consider their duties completed at the evening hour of five o'clock, at which time they may return to their various homes.

---

1. _____

2. _____

D. Changes in Word Meanings

Mrs. White agreed with the rules in Mr. White's memo, but she felt that the memo was too wordy. She wants the memo rewritten so it is brief and clear. On the lines below, rewrite the memo in a way that would please Mrs. White.

_____

_____

_____

_____

_____

_____

Name _____

Critical Thinking, Gray Level. © 1987 Steck-Vaughn Co.

ANALYZING

Analyzing means seeing how parts fit together.
Look at the picture of the train car. Can you tell
what's inside? What clues helped you interpret this
picture? Did the straw inside the car give you a clue?
Did the letters on the train help you? Name some
other things that are probably carried in cars on
this train.

When you prepare a report, you look for information that provides you with specific facts. Including important facts in your report helps make it complete.

Suppose that you are preparing a report on the Erie Canal. In three different sources, you find the three paragraphs below. Read the paragraphs. Then follow the instructions below them.

1.   The Erie Canal was needed when it was built in the early 1800s. The canal went across the Mohawk Valley, which did not have many settlers. The canal was a success from the start.

2.   Most settlers lived in the eastern United States in the early 1800s. A canal was needed to help the people move West. A route was surveyed in 1810, and the canal was completed in 1825. It connected Lake Erie with the ocean. Traffic flourished until about 1900.

3.   A canal trip was an exciting undertaking in the early days of our country. Migrating westward by way of the Erie Canal was a thrill unmatched. Many strange and beautiful sights unfolded before those who traveled aboard one of the Erie's horse-drawn barges.

A. Circle the paragraph that gives the most helpful information.

B. List the facts contained in the paragraph you chose. You should be able to list five facts if your listing is adequate and complete.

1. _____

2. _____

3. _____

4. _____

5. _____

Name _____

Critical Thinking, Gray Level. © 1987 Steck-Vaughn Co.

When you are asked to perform a task, you need certain details in order to do the task correctly and efficiently. Imagine that you are in the following situations. Tell what you need to know before you can complete each task well.

1. You work in a department store. A customer asks for a bicycle wheel. You need to

   know _____

   _____

   _____

2. You work in a hardware store. A customer wants a new lawn mower and would

   like to have it delivered. You need to know _____

   _____

   _____

3. Your school principal has asked your class to organize a school art show. Your class

   needs to know _____

   _____

   _____

4. Your teacher has asked you to write a composition. You need to know _____

   _____

   _____

5. Your parents have asked you to help organize a birthday party for a younger child.

   You need to know _____

   _____

   _____

Name _____

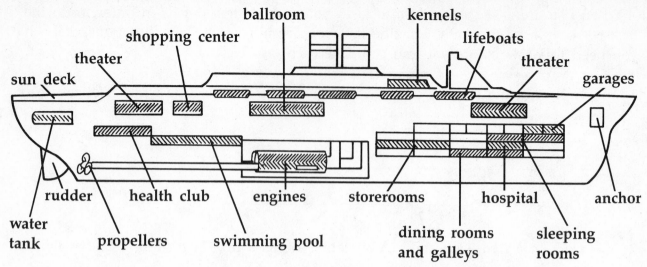

Cruise ships, or ocean liners, are huge seagoing hotels. There are often as many as a thousand workers, or crew, aboard to provide for the comfort, safety, and health of the passengers. Ocean liners can travel 10,000 miles without stopping for fuel, water, or supplies. Their galleys, or kitchens, can prepare meals which serve 9,000 daily.

Study the drawing of an ocean liner and read the paragraph. The sentences below refer to the drawing. Put **T** before each sentence which is true according to the drawing. Put **F** before each sentence which is not true according to the drawing.

_____ 1. There is a place to get a haircut on the ship.

_____ 2. The drawing shows where the fuel is stored.

_____ 3. Two people could attend different movies at the same time.

_____ 4. Passengers may transport their cars across the ocean on this ship.

_____ 5. There are escape boats for the passengers in case of emergency.

_____ 6. The swimming pool is on the sun deck.

_____ 7. There is a special place for people who become ill.

_____ 8. Passengers may bring their dogs on this voyage.

_____ 9. There is a flight deck where planes can land on the ship.

Name

Critical Thinking, Gray Level. © 1987 Steck-Vaughn Co.

When information is **relevant**, it is important to the subject you are studying. **Relevant** information is to the point.

For each activity below, underline the **two** information sources that would provide you with the most relevant information.

1. You want to find a recipe for upside-down cake.
   recipe book   cookbook   magazine   newspaper

2. You want to know how to bandage a deep cut.
   magazine   science book   health book   first aid book

3. You would like to learn how to grow zinnias.
   gardening book   book on shrubs   book on soil
   instructions on a package of zinnia seeds

4. You need to know the names of the planets in our solar system.
   health book   astronomy book   astrology book   science book

5. You want to know how to spell and pronounce the word **pecuniary**.
   atlas   spelling book   dictionary   newspaper

6. You would like to become informed about different careers.
   social studies book   individual books describing careers
   newspaper articles   counseling books

7. You need to improve your handwriting.
   chart on cursive letters   spelling book   English book
   handwriting book

8. You are interested in the duties of nurses.
   hospital manual   health book   book about careers
   book of medical diseases

9. You are interested in the most recent scientific discoveries.
   science book   newspaper   encyclopedia   recent science magazines

10. You want to know how to install rear speakers in your car.
    book about engines   car owner's manual
    printed instructions that come with new speakers

Name

Suppose that you are to write a report about life in the Amazon region of South America. From the 12 sentences below, choose the ten that you think are most relevant to the subject. Then organize the ten sentences into a paragraph, rewording where necessary.

1. Malaria is more common in tropical areas than in other places.
2. Mosquito netting is necessary equipment in this region.
3. Due to flooding and poor soil, the region does not have good farmland.
4. The temperature stays between 70°F and 90°F.
5. The sun can cause serious sunburn even on a cloudy day.
6. Tropical rainfall is heavy and frequent.
7. Tropical rivers contain anacondas, alligators, and piranha.
8. The climate of equatorial regions is hot and humid all year.
9. Salt tablets may help to maintain body fluids in hot climates.
10. Boiling is one way to purify water for drinking.
11. A great variety of trees and plants grow in the Amazon region.
12. Here in this equatorial region the chief mode of travel is by boat along the Amazon River.

Name _____

Critical Thinking, Gray Level. © 1987 Steck-Vaughn Co.

Groups of words that name related objects can be ranked from **abstract** to **concrete**. Usually a word that names a **particular** person or object is most **concrete**. Words become more abstract as they name categories that include more and more objects or people.

A. In each sentence below, there are four words or word groups that are related. Study the sentence and underline these related words or word groups. Then write **1** over the word or word group that is most abstract. Use the numerals **2**, **3**, and **4** over the other words as you narrow them down to the most concrete. The first sentence has been done for you.

1.   4   3   2
    Mrs. Smith was voted the best teacher of all the personnel

                                         1
    working in our school system.

2. Henry Aaron was one of the best home-run hitters of all the

    batters who have been major league baseball players.

3. Dogs are among our favorite household pets, and the golden retriever

    is perhaps the favorite kind of hunting dog.

4. Among the trees chosen for yards, the maple is one of the most

    popular, and the red maple is one of the most spectacular of plants.

B. Rewrite each sentence below, replacing the underlined words with ones that are more concrete.

1. He went into the room and prepared a meal. _____

    _____

2. She got into the vehicle and headed for the roadway. _____

    _____

3. We put the liquid into a container. _____

    _____

Name

Good writers usually try to use concrete words and phrases as much as possible. Such words and phrases help the reader see, understand, and analyze what the writer is telling about.

A. Read the following paragraph. Underline the concrete words and phrases that help you to see what the writer is telling about.

One summer evening while I was sitting on the verandah of our rambling old house in Riverdale, I saw a dark object sail downward through the dusk toward the base of a White Ash that stood about twenty feet away on the lawn. I heard a soft **plop** as the object landed. There was just enough light for me to see that it was a Flying Squirrel that had landed head-upward on the trunk of the tree just a few feet above the ground. Then it shot up the tree like a streak and disappeared.

—from *A Natural History of New York City* by John Kieran

B. Write a concrete word or word group from the paragraph above that can replace each abstract term in the list below.

1. a sound _____

4. a distance _____

2. a tree _____

5. an animal _____

3. a town _____

6. a time of day_____

C. Write a brief description of an animal—wild or domestic—that you have observed. Use as many concrete words and phrases as possible to make your description vivid to your readers.

_____

_____

_____

_____

_____

_____

Name _____

Critical Thinking, Gray Level. © 1987 Steck-Vaughn Co.

Actions are **logical** if they **make sense** in helping you to achieve a specific goal.

A. Suppose that you are the oldest of three children. Your sister is six and your brother is four. Your parents have asked that the three of you do the following chores before they return home from work. Write **sister**, **brother**, or **myself** after each chore to show the logical person you would assign to each job.

1. pick up toys _____

2. rake leaves _____

3. walk the dog _____

4. feed the cat _____

5. carry out the garbage _____

6. take the grocery list and go to the store _____

7. vacuum the living room rug _____

8. renew some books from the library _____

9. get the mail from the mailbox _____

10. polish the children's shoes _____

B. Suppose that it is holiday time. You have saved $16 with which to buy gifts for the following people: your parents, a younger brother or sister, a grandparent, your best friend. On the lines below, list in order at least five logical steps you would take before and during your shopping trip.

1. _____

2. _____

3. _____

4. _____

5. _____

Name

A. Parking places were difficult to find, even in 1926. In that year, someone invented a lightweight car which had a set of small wheels at the back. To park the car, a person stood it up on these wheels. Was this a logical solution to the parking

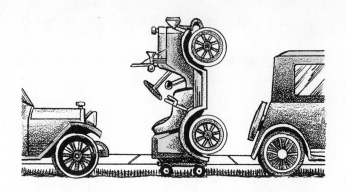

problem? _____

Why or why not? _____

_____

Could we use this kind of solution to today's parking problems? _____

Why or why not? _____

_____

_____

B. Two classes were planning a trip. They found three possible places to go. Their problem was that the classes could not choose which one they liked best. Finally, Rosa suggested that the teachers break the deadlock by choosing a different place from the three the students had suggested.

Was this a logical plan? _____

Why or why not? _____

_____

On the lines below, write a logical suggestion of your own to solve the classes' problem.

_____

_____

_____

_____

Name

Critical Thinking, Gray Level. © 1987 Steck-Vaughn Co.

One important **element**, or **part**, of a story is the **setting**. The setting is **where** the story takes place. A good description of a setting can help you analyze why the story characters feel and act as they do. The description can also give you, the reader, a special feeling—such as comfort, fear, curiosity, or happiness.

The setting of the book *Charlotte's Web* is a farm. The paragraph below describes a very special part of that setting. Read the paragraph and write answers to the questions that follow it.

> The barn was very large. It was very old. It smelled of hay and it smelled of manure. It smelled of the perspiration of tired horses and the wonderful sweet breath of patient cows. It often had a sort of peaceful smell—as though nothing bad could happen ever again in the world. It smelled of grain and of harness dressing and of axle grease and of rubber boots and of new rope. And whenever the cat was given a fish-head to eat, the barn would smell of fish. But mostly it smelled of hay, for there was always hay in the great loft up overhead. And there was always hay being pitched down to the cows and the horses and the sheep.

1. Would you enjoy being in the place described above? _____

   Explain why or why not? _____

   _____

   _____

2. Which word in the selection gives you the most important characteristic of the barn?

   _____ Why does the author use that word so frequently?

   _____

   _____

3. Suppose the author had decided to use the sense of **hearing** as the basis for describing the setting of the barn. What details might such a paragraph include?

   _____

   _____

   _____

Name _____

Most American folktales are based on the adventures of real people. Therefore, folktales have an **element of reality** in them. However, as folktales were retold through the years, **elements of fantasy** were added.

Read the folktale below. Then answer the questions.

His real name was Jonathan Chapman. As a young man, he set a strange and wonderful goal for himself. He wanted to carry apple seeds from the orchards of the eastern United States to the cleared lands in the West. His dream was to see the fragrant, lovely, productive apple orchards blooming for the western settlers, too.

Carrying sacks of apple seeds on his back, Chapman made journeys to western Pennsylvania and to the river valleys of Ohio and Indiana. He gave the seeds to home builders along the frontier. As Chapman's journeys and the stories about him spread, it was natural that he soon became known as Johnny Appleseed.

Johnny Appleseed dedicated his life to his task. There was no way for him to grow rich. As an old man, he wore a tin pot on his head to protect him from the rain and snow, for he could not afford to buy a hat. He made his clothing out of old sacks.

Wherever he went, Johnny was loved and respected. Native Americans considered him a brother, for he shared their love of nature. Even wild animals considered him their friend. Bears let him play freely with their cubs. Shy animals, such as deer and wolves, came close to him, unafraid. Even dangerous animals, such as wildcats, knew enough to let Johnny pass by unharmed.

A. List three facts about Jonathan Chapman.

1. _____

2. _____

3. _____

B. List any parts of the story that you consider fanciful.

_____

_____

_____

C. Choose one of the parts you listed in Activity B. Explain why you consider this to

be a fanciful element of the story. _____

_____

Name

Critical Thinking, Gray Level. © 1987 Steck-Vaughn Co.

A story is **logical** if it is told in an order that makes sense. Usually this order relates to time. The author begins with what happened first and ends with what happened last.

A. The outline below is not written in the correct time sequence. Rewrite the outline on the blank lines so that the sequence is correct.

Charles Dodgson

II. Later life

    A. Wrote *Alice in Wonderland*

    B. Died in 1898

    C. Took the pen name Lewis Carroll

I. Early life

    A. Teacher of mathematics

    B. Born in 1832

Charles Dodgson

I. Early life

_____

_____

_____

_____

_____

_____

B. Use your rewritten outline to write a short paragraph about the life of Charles Dodgson. Keep the facts in the correct sequence.

_____

_____

_____

_____

_____

_____

Name _____

Seven sentence parts are listed in the box. Decide where each sentence part fits logically within the article, and write it in the blank.

```
1. act as cleanup squads for debris      5. three body segments
2. two pairs of wings                    6. outer skeletons
3. three-fourths of all animal life      7. provide food
4. climate and food supply
```

An insect is an animal with an outside skeleton, a shell-like covering, and usually

_____. An adult insect has six legs, and its

appendages have joints. Insects have _____

These are the head, thorax, and abdomen.

Our world is teeming with insects. Insects comprise about _____

_____ on our planet. Though most insects are tiny and live less than

a year, they have not become extinct for several reasons. They have adapted to changes

in _____; they are able to reproduce quickly;

their bodies are protected by _____; and they are able

to escape danger by flying.

While many kinds of insects are harmful, other kinds are useful. Insects _____

_____ for birds, fish, and other small animals. Insects also

pollinate plants and _____

DRAGONFLY   **TERMITE**   **BUTTERFLY**

Name

Critical Thinking, Gray Level. © 1987 Steck-Vaughn Co.

A **fallacy** is an error in reasoning. Be on the lookout for fallacies in **either-or** statements. An **either-or** statement says that only two choices are possible. Sometimes this is true. For example, **You are either in school or not in school**. Often, however, there are other choices possible besides the two in an either-or statement.

Each statement below is an **either-or** fallacy. Change each one so that it is **not** a fallacy. The first one is done for you.

1. People have either dogs or cats for pets. _____

    People may have dogs, cats, birds, hamsters, and many other kinds

    of animals as pets.

2. Either it is raining or the sun is shining. _____

_____

_____

3. A person is either your friend or your enemy. _____

_____

_____

4. Water is contained in either lakes or bays. _____

_____

_____

5. Fish may be eaten either with butter or with lemon. _____

_____

_____

6. Either you play with a group or you don't play at all. _____

_____

_____

Name _____

Another kind of fallacy is the **slanted argument**. In a slanted argument, the writer or speaker presents information in a way that is meant to convince you to think or act in a certain way. Here are some methods used in slanted arguments:

1. **Use of glad words:** words that make you feel positive and enthusiastic about a person or a product.

2. **Bandwagon technique:** statements that try to make you feel that "everyone else" is doing something, so you should, too.

3. **Famous-person endorsement:** statements that well-known public figures support an idea or use a product.

A. Read each slanted argument below. Then write the number of the slanted argument method that is being used.

   1. All across the nation, it's the Lemon-Aid generation! _____

   2. Rock star Emmy Emerald eats Raisin Cane Cereal every day! _____

   3. This soft, velvety cream makes skin feel silky smooth. _____

   4. Vote Row A on Election Day to get fair play and honesty in government. _____

   5. Smart families rely on Safety Swoop Sirens. How about your family? _____

B. For each sentence below, choose and write the phrase that would probably make the best slanted argument out of the sentence.

   1.   ask for   insist on   are interested in

       People in-the-know _____ Mo-Go Motor Oil.

   2.   many Americans   hungry people   actor Lance Lotmore

       Bit-o-Burger is the quick meal preferred by _____

   3.   adventure-filled   very nice   safe and quiet

       To drive the Galaxy 2000 is to have a new, _____ experience.

Name _____

Critical Thinking, Gray Level. © 1987 Steck-Vaughn Co.

A true **analogy** is a statement which shows the relationship between two pairs of words. The first pair of words shows what the relationship is about. Here are some examples:

- **Up** is to **down** as **over** is to **under**. (Relationship: opposites)
- **Second** is to **minute** as **hour** is to **day**. (Relationship: part of)
- **Clock** is to **time** as **scale** is to **weight**. (Relationship: function)

A. Write **opposite**, **part of**, or **function** after each analogy.

   1. **Ounce** is to **pound** as **inch** is to **foot**. _____

   2. **Saw** is to **cut** as **shovel** is to **dig**. _____

   3. **In** is to **out** as **beautiful** is to **ugly**. _____

B. Make each analogy true by choosing the correct word to complete it.

   1. **Rug** is to **floor** as **blanket** is to _____.
                                            warm   bed   wool

   2. **Needle** is to **sew** as **hammer** is to _____.
                                            metal   tool   hit

   3. **Shy** is to **bold** as **quiet** is to _____.
                                            loud   silent   sleep

C. The analogies below are false, because the last word in each one is incorrect. That is, the last word does not continue to show the relationship set up in the first pair of words. Cross out the last word. On the line, write the word that will make the analogy true.

   1. **Scissors** are to **cut** as **rulers** are to **color**. _____

   2. **Foot** is to **leg** as **hand** is to **body**. _____

   3. **Happy** is to **sad** as **fast** is to **quick**. _____

   4. **Pencil** is to **writing** as **brush** is to **comb**. _____

   5. **Car** is to **drive** as **airplane** is to **wing**. _____

Name _____

An **assumption** is an idea we reach before we have all the facts. Some assumptions turn out to be true. Others, however, turn out to be false. When all the facts are gathered, the assumption may prove to be wrong.

Read each item below. On line **1** make an assumption about the situation. On line **2** write why the assumption may be wrong.

A. A man climbs up a fire-escape and opens a window to an apartment.

    1. _____

    2. _____

B. Amy plays the tuba. She decides to try out for the school band. On the day of the tryouts, Amy sees a long line of students waiting by the band room. Amy goes home.

    1. _____

    2. _____

C. Don grabbed the lunch bag and hurried to the cafeteria. As he began eating, Clark came over. "That's my lunch," said Clark. "My name is written on the bottom of the bag." Clark turned the bag over. There was the name **Clark**.

    1. _____

    2. _____

D. Sara was not doing well at school. She daydreamed in class. She seldom completed her homework. She was not willing to participate in class activities. When called on, her answers were usually wrong.

    1. _____

    2. _____

Name _____

Critical Thinking, Gray Level. © 1987 Steck-Vaughn Co.

A Elements of a Selection

Read the poem. Then do the activities that follow it.

The Bird of Night

A shadow is floating through the moonlight.
Its wings don't make a sound.
Its claws are long, its beak is bright.
Its eyes try all the corners of the night.

It calls and calls: all the air swells and heaves
And washes up and down like water.
The ear that listens to the owl believes
In death. The bat beneath the eaves,

The mouse beside the stone are still as death —
The owl's air washes them like water.
The owl goes back and forth inside the night,
And the night holds its breath.   —Randall Jarrell

1. What is the **setting** described in the poem? _____

2. Name the main character in the poem. _____

3. Is the main character real or fanciful? _____

B Judging Completeness

List three phrases from the poem that help make the description of the owl complete.

1. _____

2. _____

3. _____

C Logic of Actions

Why is it **logical** that the bat and the mouse stay very still as the owl flies by?

_____

Name _____

D. Recognizing Fallacies
    Story Logic
    Abstract or Concrete
    Relevance of Information

Read the person's words. Then follow the directions that tell you how to rewrite the person's statement.

1. Rewrite the statement so that it is not an **either-or** fallacy.

_____

_____

2. Rewrite the statement so that it tells logically what the children are watching.

_____

_____

3. Rewrite the statement so that the words **These birds** are replaced by more concrete words.

_____

_____

4. Rewrite the statement so that it tells where to find relevant information about myna birds.

_____

_____

Name

_____

Critical Thinking, Gray Level. © 1987 Steck-Vaughn Co.

SYNTHESIZING

Synthesizing means putting information together to come up with new ideas. Look at the picture of the young man. What is he doing? Is this a dangerous sport? Why or why not? Why do you think the young man is wearing a life jacket? Name some other water sports that are similar to this one.

A **concept** is a general idea we have about an object or a process. For example, the concept we have about **written information** is that it will be presented to us in fully spelled-out words and complete sentences. Sometimes, however, written information is presented in an **abbreviated** form. In such cases, you have to adjust your thinking so that you can understand the message.

In the following classified advertisements from a newspaper, the information is abbreviated. Study each advertisement. Then rewrite it in sentence form with the words fully spelled out.

1.

> FURNITURE SALE—Auto washer, 14 cu. ft.
> 2 dr refrig, b & w TV, 4 pc BR set, 5 pc din set,
> misc lamps. E–Z terms.

_____

_____

_____

_____

_____

2.

> NEED EXEC SECY—typ 70 wpm, shthnd, fil.
> Local ofc of nat'l co. Paid hosp ins, 2 wk vac, top
> hrly pay. 40 hr wk. Apply 8–5, M–F.

_____

_____

_____

_____

_____

Name _____

Critical Thinking, Gray Level. © 1987 Steck-Vaughn Co.

A map, like the one below, can give you a fast visual idea of how water and land are related in space. Study the map. Notice where smaller rivers join to form larger rivers with new names.

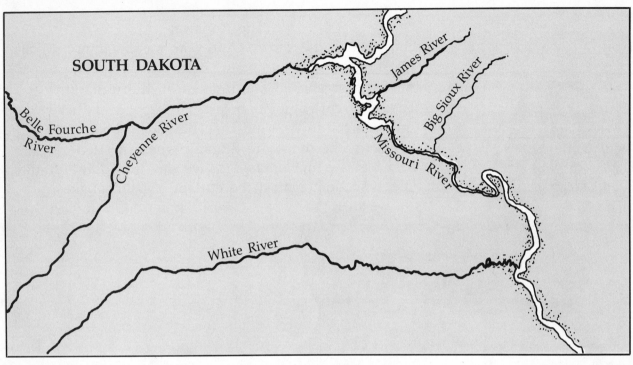

A. On the lines below, write a paragraph that describes the river system shown in the map.

_____

_____

_____

_____

B. Which type of communication—the map or the paragraph—makes it easier to

understand the river system? _____

Tell why you think so. _____

_____

Name _____

Artists and writers present the same idea in different ways. Study the statue of a horse. Then read the selection from a poem which tells about a special kind of horse, the Morgan. Write answers to the questions which follow the picture and the poem.

The Runaway

Once, when the snow of the year was beginning to fall,
We stopped by a mountain pasture to say, "Whose colt?"
A little Morgan had one forefoot on the wall,
The other curled at his breast. He dipped his head
And snorted to us. And then he had to bolt.
We heard the miniature thunder where he fled
And we saw him or thought we saw him dim and gray,
Like a shadow against the curtain of falling flakes.

—Robert Frost

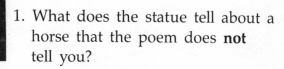

1. What does the statue tell about a horse that the poem does **not** tell you?

_____

_____

2. What does the **poem** about a horse tell you that the statue **cannot** tell you?

_____

_____

Name

Critical Thinking, Gray Level. © 1987 Steck-Vaughn Co.

To plan and complete a project usually requires lots of time. It may also involve many people doing specific jobs.

Suppose that the HomeLife Corporation has decided to build a housing project. The company has bought a hundred acres of land, which will be subdivided into one-half acre plots. On each plot, a home will be built. The list below names some of the workers who will be needed on the project. Tell what each worker's specific job will be. You may use a dictionary.

1. surveyor _____

_____

2. architect _____

_____

3. landscape designer _____

_____

4. contractor _____

_____

5. road crew _____

_____

6. interior designer _____

_____

7. real estate salespeople _____

_____

8. model-home staff _____

_____

9. zoning-board member _____

_____

Name

Suppose that your class has been asked to plan a talent show for all the pupils in Grades 1 through 6. In the show, there must be several performers from each classroom. The principal has asked that the show be approximately one-and-a-half hours long.

You have one month to prepare for the show. On the lines below, list specific jobs that must be assigned to people in your class, such as **talent scout** and **director**. Briefly tell what the person holding that job must do.

1. _____

_____

_____

2. _____

_____

_____

3. _____

_____

_____

4. _____

_____

_____

5. _____

_____

_____

Name

Critical Thinking, Gray Level. © 1987 Steck-Vaughn Co.

Even if you plan a project carefully, you may find that some step along the way cannot be carried out as you wanted it to be. In such cases, you must think of **another** way to complete the step.

Study each situation below. Then tell how the pupil might solve the problem in order to get the step done.

1. For social studies, Marilyn is conducting a project about community history. She is interviewing older citizens to find out what the community was like in years gone by. Marilyn uses a tape recorder as she interviews each person. Mrs. Z. is willing to be interviewed, but she does not want to speak into a tape recorder. How can Marilyn complete the interview?

_____

_____

_____

2. For science, Luis plans to make a relief map showing the different rock formations in his state. Ms. Frank, a geologist, had agreed to help Luis with his project, but now she cannot do that, because she must attend a conference in Europe. There seem to be no other local geologists whom Luis can consult. What do you think he should do?

_____

_____

_____

3. For a language arts project, Susan has collected jump-rope rhymes and other game rhymes used by children in her community. She planned to type all the rhymes on pages for a *Game Rhyme Magazine* and have the pages copied on a photocopy machine. Now Susan has learned that the school photocopier is broken. She cannot afford to pay for copies made at a shop. How can Susan get her *Game Rhyme Magazine* put together for her classmates?

_____

_____

Name _____

A. Think about the following projects. Underline the one that you would prefer to carry out.

1. Show the effect of temperature and light on the growth of bean seeds.

2. Make a floor plan and model of the ideal school.

3. Identify ten birds common to your area by making drawings and recording the different birdcalls.

B. Complete the following lists to show how you would begin the project you selected in part A.

Supplies Needed

1. _____   4. _____

2. _____   5. _____

3. _____   6. _____

Five Major Steps to Take

1. _____

2. _____

3. _____

4. _____

5. _____

People to Consult or Ask for Help

1. _____

2. _____

Name _____

Critical Thinking, Gray Level. © 1987 Steck-Vaughn Co.

A **hypothesis** is a beginning explanation of what is happening or why something happened. A hypothesis may change as new facts are gathered.

The true story below is given in three parts. Read each part and answer the question that follows it. Then continue reading the story.

1.   In the summer of 1890, millionaire Harry Lehr invited his friends to a dinner party. His friends were excited because he told them that a very special guest would be there. Mr. Lehr's wealthy friends were used to important people, but they were curious about the identity of this special guest.

Who do you think the guest might be?

_____

2.   As the special guest entered the room, the other guests gasped in surprise. It was the Prince del Drago! He was attired elegantly in a black suit and tie. During dinner, however, the Prince did not talk to anyone. Silently, he ate his dinner.

Why do you think this special guest was silent?

_____

3.   When he finished eating, the Prince left the table and jumped to the huge chandelier. Then he unscrewed the light bulbs and threw them crashing down onto the table.

Circle the picture below that identifies the Prince del Drago. On the lines below the pictures, tell what facts in the story led you to this hypothesis.

_____

_____

_____

Name _____

A. Five hypotheses and ten statements are listed below. Each hypothesis can be supported by facts. Which statements provide the facts that support each hypothesis? Write the letter of each statement before the hypothesis it supports. You will use more than one statement to support each hypothesis.

Hypotheses

_____ 1. Insecticides are not necessarily a sure way to kill mosquitoes.

_____ 2. The bathtub is one of the most dangerous areas in the home.

_____ 3. Some people dislike poetry.

_____ 4. Typewritten papers usually receive higher grades than handwritten papers.

_____ 5. Driver-training courses contribute to highway safety.

Statements

a. The hard material can cause broken bones and severe bruises.

b. Often it was not a part of their early learning.

c. They are easier to read.

d. Participants learn traffic laws and defensive driving attitudes.

e. There is proof that areas frequently sprayed still have many insects.

f. The enamel surface is so slippery that one can fall easily.

g. Driver-training graduates have fewer accidents than untrained drivers.

h. Some mosquitoes fly out of range of the spray.

i. Perhaps the subject was not presented in an interesting manner.

j. They have a more professional look.

B. Choose one of the hypotheses above. Write another statement to support it.

_____

Name

Critical Thinking, Gray Level. © 1987 Steck-Vaughn Co.

Read the selection below. Then answer the questions that follow it.

Frédéric Chopin, the Polish composer, was visiting a friend in France—a woman named George Sand. As Chopin and Sand talked, they watched in delight as Sand's little dog raced around the room, chasing its tail, rolling on its back, and pursuing imaginary cats and mice. The puppy became exhausted and flopped to rest for a few seconds. Then it got up and began its wild games again.

Chopin laughed. He walked to the piano. Quickly he put together a composition which seemed to whirl and circle. Midway in the composition, Chopin put in a quiet part in which the music seemed to rest. Then the music picked up speed again. This piano composition—put together in such a happy spirit and with very little pre-planning—became one of Chopin's most famous piano pieces. It is known as "The Minute Waltz."

1. What inspired Chopin to write "The Minute Waltz"?

_____

2. What facts in the story led you to make the hypothesis you stated in item 1?

_____

_____

3. In what ways does "The Minute Waltz" reflect the movements of the little dog?

_____

_____

4. Musicians get their ideas from many sources. On the basis of the facts in the story above, what hypothesis can you make about one of these sources?

_____

_____

Name

89

A. Three situations are described below. Write two hypotheses to explain each situation.

   1. A circus truck stops at a baseball field.

      a. _____

      _____

      b. _____

   2. A stranger gets into your teacher's car and drives away.

      a. _____

      _____

      b. _____

B. 1. Choose one of the hypotheses you wrote for part A and copy it below.

   _____

   _____

   2. Now list three facts you would need in order to show that your hypothesis is a valid, or true, one.

      a. _____

      b. _____

      c. _____

Name

Critical Thinking, Gray Level. © 1987 Steck-Vaughn Co.

A **conclusion** is a final statement you can make based on the facts given to you. Read the articles below. Make a check by each conclusion that could **not** be made from the facts given in the article.

A.   Soil may be described as the earth's cover where the land stops and the air begins. Every ounce of fertile soil normally contains more living organisms than the human population of the entire world.

    The soil provides a very effective sewage and waste disposal system. Earth's materials are recycled in the soil as life goes through generation after generation. It is unfortunate that much soil has been damaged through misuse, erosion, and the use of harmful chemicals.

_____ 1. Even poor soil is full of living things.

_____ 2. Good soil contributes to the cycle of life on Earth.

_____ 3. The earth's surface is covered with soil.

_____ 4. People have deliberately damaged the soil.

_____ 5. Scientists have carefully studied soil.

B.   On May 25, 1961, President John Kennedy announced that the U.S. would land a person on the moon before the end of the decade. This tremendous mission cost $24 billion. The goal was finally reached when Apollo 11 landed on the moon's surface on July 20, 1969. Neil Armstrong, Edwin Aldrin, and Michael Collins were on board Apollo 11. Armstrong and Aldrin spent twenty-one hours and thirty-seven minutes on the moon before returning to the command ship.

_____ 1. Three astronauts walked on the moon.

_____ 2. The Apollo trip was costly.

_____ 3. President Kennedy was interested in the trip to the moon.

_____ 4. Several people wanted to go on the moon mission.

_____ 5. The astronauts faced incredible dangers.

Name _____

You can reach conclusions by carefully studying a picture or a scene. Each conclusion below can be reached by putting together various details shown in the illustration. Write the facts that lead to each conclusion.

1. There are five people in the family.

_____

2. One family member is about three or four years old.

_____

3. Someone in the family uses a wheelchair.

_____

4. The family has at least two pets.

_____

5. It is springtime.

_____

_____

Name

Critical Thinking, Gray Level. © 1987 Steck-Vaughn Co.

If you understand someone's personality, you can often conclude what he or she will do in a certain situation. The pupils described below must take part in a class play. Read about each pupil. Then tell what particular task the pupil is likely to volunteer to do in the play.

1. Dirk is extremely shy. He is, however, interested in watching plays, movies, and television dramas. It is not the actors that interest Dirk so much as it is the lighting and sound effects used in the productions.

2. Carla seems to have a special gift for working with color. Her friends always admire her paintings. She dresses in an original way. She has a knack for combining her clothes so that she always looks very special.

3. Mario is a great talker. He likes to tell jokes and is always ready to give colorful descriptions of things that have happened to him. Even from a distance, you can always identify Mario's voice, which rings with laughter.

4. Francine has a collection of notebooks in which she is always writing. One notebook is a journal about her personal experiences. Another notebook contains Francine's story ideas. In still another notebook, Francine lists interesting words she finds as she reads or as she listens to people talk.

5. When pupils are arguing over what game to play or what project to carry out, they very often call on Marta to settle the dispute. She has a way of solving problems and organizing activities that makes her classmates like and respect her.

Dirk's job in the play:

_____

Carla's job in the play:

_____

Mario's job in the play:

_____

Francine's job in the play:

_____

Marta's job in the play:

_____

Name

_____

In the script of a play, the dialogue and the directions (in parentheses) help you draw conclusions about the characters. Read the following part of a script. Then answer the questions.

Ariel   *(shaking slightly)*: I do not want to cross this foggy swamp! At night it is filled with goblins and other dreadful creatures. ***(She pulls away from Cassie.)***

Cassie   *(extending her hand to Ariel)*: Oh, come along, Ariel! Don't be such a fearful thing. There is magic that will protect us. And besides, we must cross the swamp and rescue the Prince before the sun rises.

Ariel   *(moving toward Cassie again)*: Oh, yes. The Prince! We can't break our promise to him. But what is the magic, Cassie? What do you mean when you say **magic**?

Cassie   *(smiling)*: If you will come with me, Ariel, you will see that the magic is inside you. The name of the magic begins with the letter **C**. Now do come along!

Ariel   *(taking Cassie's hand)*: The letter **C**. . .what could that be? **Calm**? **Curiosity**? **Caring**? Oh, this is all too scary and puzzling for me! *(Ariel and Cassie move into the foggy swamp as the howl of the Swamp Goblin fills the air.)*

1. What kind of person is Ariel? _____

_____

2. What kind of person is Cassie? _____

_____

3. Does this play tell a story of fantasy or a story of reality? _____

     How do you know? _____

4. Imagine that Ariel and Cassie are now in the middle of the swamp. Write another line of dialogue for each character.

_____

_____

_____

Name

Critical Thinking, Gray Level. © 1987 Steck-Vaughn Co.

One day Samantha announced to her friends that she was a math wizard. "To prove this," said Samantha, "I want each of you to follow these steps:

1. Write a three-digit number in which the first and last digit differ by at least 2.

2. Reverse the digits in your number and write the new number.

3. You should now have two three-digit numbers. Subtract the smaller number from the larger one. Write down your answer.

4. Reverse the digits in your answer and write the new number.

5. Add this new number to your answer in step 3."

After Samatha's friends finished, Samantha whispered to each of them, "Your final answer is 1089." In each case, Samantha was absolutely right!

A. What is your conclusion about Samantha's magic trick?

_____

_____

B. On the lines below, test your conclusion by following steps 1 through 5 as given above.

_____

_____

_____

_____

C. Check your conclusion again by asking a classmate or your teacher to carry out the steps.

D. Suppose your classmate or teacher comes up with an answer that is not 1089. What will your conclusion be?

_____

_____

Name _____

Read the following passage from a book. Then answer the questions.

Fire!

In that instant Murchison pressed the button of the ignition device, thereby establishing the current and hurling an electric spark into the depths of the cannon. A terrible, thunderlike detonation ensued, the likes of which had never been heard before, with such roaring and flashing that it exceeded anything imaginable. A huge column of fire shot out from the ground as from a crater. The earth trembled; some of the spectators momentarily caught sight of the projectile, as it triumphantly shot through fiery vapors up into the atmosphere. The streak of white-hot flame which rose to the heavens spread its light over all of Florida. . .

from *Journey from the Earth to the Moon* by Jules Verne

1. The author of the passage was making a living as a poet, playwright, and accountant. He had, however, become bored in the company of poets, actors, and bankers. So he began to visit the library frequently, studying another subject which interested him. What do you conclude that the subject was?

_____

_____

2. The passage was written by Jules Verne and comes from his book *Journey from the Earth to the Moon*. The book was published in 1863. Some of Verne's other books are *Twenty Thousand Leagues Under the Sea*, *Journey to the Center of the Earth*, and *The Mysterious Island*. What kind of books do you conclude that these are?

_____

3. Jules Verne became known as "the man who invented the future." From this nickname, what do you conclude about the things Verne told about in his books?

_____

_____

Name

Critical Thinking, Gray Level. © 1987 Steck-Vaughn Co.

There is usually more than one way to solve a problem. When you offer another solution, you are **proposing an alternative**. Read each item below. Then propose an alternative to the solution given.

1. Your teacher tells you to measure a distance in meters but you can find only a yardstick. You decide that measuring the distance in yards is better than not measuring it at all.

_____

_____

2. You lost a button on your shirt. To keep your shirt closed, you fastened it with a safety pin. Now the pin is making a tear in your shirt.

_____

_____

3. Your class is giving a play. Five students have volunteered for the leading role. One student says he should be given the part because he did well in the last class play.

_____

_____

4. Your class has a new word game. The game is played with two teams. Ten players are needed on each team. Since there are twenty-two students in your class, you tell two of your classmates that they will have to be left out of the game.

_____

_____

5. You have worked hard to prepare your oral book report. Today is the big day! All of a sudden you discover that you left your notes at home. You decide to give your report without your notes even though you know that it won't be very good.

_____

_____

Name _____

There are many alternate ways to study the words on a spelling list. Try the two ways described below.

A. In each word on your spelling list, find as many smaller words as you can. The rule is that the letters of the smaller word must appear in the same order as they do in the whole word.

   Here is an example: In the word **innocent** you can find the smaller words **in**, **inn**, **no**, and **cent**. In each spelling word below, find and write at least two other words.

   1. doctorate _____

   2. mayoral _____

   3. grind _____

   4. operation _____

   5. detestable _____

   6. carefully _____

   7. satisfactory _____

   8. twine _____

   9. countryside _____

B. An alternate way of studying spelling words is to make **letter-block-pictures** of each word. If the letter is short, make a block that sits **on** the line ☐———. If the letter is tall, make a block that goes up to the top line ——☐—. If the letter descends below the writing line, make a block of that shape ——☐—.

   Here is a letter-block picture of the word **mayoral**.

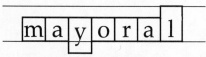

   Figure out which word in part A fits in each letter-block picture below. Write the word in the blocks.

1. ☐☐☐☐☐   2. ☐☐☐☐☐   3. ☐☐☐☐☐☐☐☐☐☐☐

Name

Critical Thinking, Gray Level. © 1987 Steck-Vaughn Co.

Study the following story and the picture that illustrates it. Then write three sentences which propose alternatives **you** might take if you actually found yourself in this situation.

One Saturday morning, as Mark walked along a seldom used path in the park, he found an expensive wrist watch on the shore of the lake. As Mark examined the watch, a man approached him.

"Give me that watch!" demanded the man. "I saw you pick it up. That watch belongs to me. Hand it over right now!"

Alternatives:

1. _____

   _____

2. _____

   _____

3. _____

   _____

Name _____

Study the situation described below. As you read, imagine that **you** are the baby-sitter.

One night, Leon accepted a job as baby-sitter for his neighbors' child, Chrissy. The first part of the evening went well. Leon fed Chrissy her supper, read her a story, and tucked her into bed. After Chrissy fell asleep, Leon went downstairs to the kitchen and started to do his homework.

Suddenly, there was a howl from Chrissy's bedroom. Leon rushed upstairs. Chrissy was holding her stomach in pain. Tears were running down her cheeks. Leon felt Chrissy's forehead. It was as hot as a firecracker!

"Hold on, Chrissy!" said Leon. He ran downstairs again to look at the telephone message pad. Chrissy's parents had forgotten to leave important information! There was no doctor's number, no number that told where Chrissy's parents could be reached, and no numbers of neighbors or friends to call.

Chrissy was sick and needed help. Leon knew that!

What are three alternatives Leon could take in this situation?

1. _____

   _____

   _____

2. _____

   _____

   _____

3. _____

   _____

   _____

Name _____

Critical Thinking, Gray Level. © 1987 Steck-Vaughn Co.

Hula hoops were once extremely popular toys. The picture shows you how they were used. Although the hula game is out-of-date now, there might still be ways to use the leftover hoops.

A. Describe how you could use a hula hoop in each case below.

1. To teach someone how to tell time

_____

_____

2. For use in a relay race, where people run from one point to another

_____

_____

3. To show social studies data, such as population groups within a certain area

_____

_____

4. To teach someone about fractions _____

_____

5. For use in an art project _____

_____

B. On the lines below, describe another use for leftover hula hoops.

_____

_____

Name _____

In the book *The Middle Moffat*, the author—Eleanor Estes—tells about Janey Moffat, the middle child in a large family. Janey has many projects. One of them is to help her neighbor, Mr. Buckle, live to be one hundred years old. Mr. Buckle is already ninety-nine years old. To help him reach his one hundredth birthday, here are some of the things that Janey Moffat does:

- She follows Mr. Buckle from a distance as he leaves the library to make sure no dogs jump on him and scare him.

- As Mr. Buckle passes the firehouse, Janey reminds him of how loud the fire siren can be, so that he will not be startled by the noise.

- Janey follows Mr. Buckle with an umbrella, just in case it may rain. She does not want him to catch cold.

- Janey does not want Mr. Buckle to trip and hurt himself. She clears the path from the library to Mr. Buckle's home by kicking aside such things as fallen branches, orange peels, and broken glass.

Suppose that you are Janey Moffat. Propose some other things you could do to help Mr. Buckle reach his one hundredth birthday.

_____

_____

_____

_____

_____

_____

_____

_____

Name _____

Critical Thinking, Gray Level. © 1987 Steck-Vaughn Co.

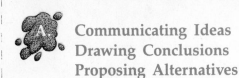 UNIT 5   EXTENDING YOUR SKILLS

A Communicating Ideas
Drawing Conclusions
Proposing Alternatives

Study the material in the boxes. Then do the activities.

Message from a Caterpillar

Don't shake this
bough.
Don't try
to wake me
now

In this cocoon
I've work to
do.
Inside this silk
I'm changing
things

I'm worm-like now
but in this
dark
I'm growing
wings.

—Lilian Moore

Four Stages in the Life of a Butterfly

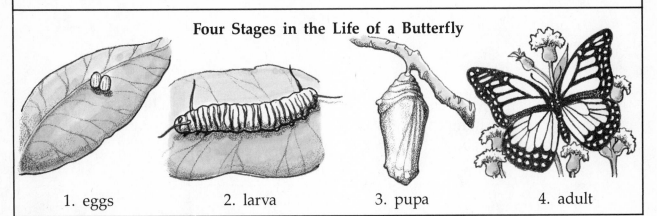

1. eggs   2. larva   3. pupa   4. adult

1. The materials above present the concept of **change**. In what two forms is the

   concept presented? _____

2. From the information given in the boxes, what insect stage do you conclude that the

   poet is telling about? _____

   What key words and phrases support your conclusions?

   _____

3. Propose an alternate way of telling about insect change. _____

   _____

Name _____

B. Building Hypotheses

The pictures at the bottom of the page show four of the many kinds of animals that migrate.

1. Write a hypothesis telling what may cause some animals to migrate.

_____

_____

2. Name some of the sources you would consult to find out whether your hypothesis is correct.

_____

_____

C. Planning Projects

Imagine that you have been asked to join an oceanographic expedition to study the migration path of the humpback whale. Describe what specific job you would like to do in this project. Tell about the materials and skills you would need.

_____

_____

_____

caribou

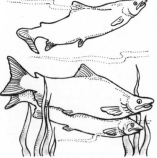
salmon

geese

whales

Name _____

Critical Thinking, Gray Level. © 1987 Steck-Vaughn Co.

EVALUATING

Evaluating means making a judgment or decision about something. Look at the picture. What has happened? How do you know? How does the picture make you feel? Why? What do you think should be done about the houses on this beach? Do you think this would be a good place to live? Why or why not?

A good **generalization** is a statement that is true for all the details that lead up to it. Read the article below. Then check each generalization that is true, according to the content of the article.

Louis had one burning desire. He wanted to become a doctor! His goal was somewhat unusual, since he was blind.

Louis attended a regular high school, where he made good grades, was on a wrestling team, and was vice-president of his class.

When he enrolled in college, the professors seemed skeptical of his ability to graduate, until Louis said that he was depending on them to prepare him for medical school. Louis graduated from college with highest honors.

Many of the medical schools to which he had applied rejected Louis. But one dean pleaded his case when he said, "I think we should let him see how far he can go."

In his third year of medical school, Louis began working with real patients. Colleagues helped him read X-rays. He could not see sore throats or skin rashes. However, he had especially acute hearing and sensitive fingers. He could hear heart abnormalities that others could not hear. He could also feel slight changes in lumps or bulges in the skin.

Louis did graduate from medical school! As one of his professors said, "Louis is not normal. He's super normal."

_____ 1. Blind people may be better at some tasks than people who have normal vision.

_____ 2. Blind people are admitted to professional schools because others feel sorry for them.

_____ 3. Blindness makes it impossible to achieve one's goals.

_____ 4. There were some things Louis could not do for his patients.

_____ 5. A blind person cannot be as successful in all aspects of a doctor's work as a sighted person.

_____ 6. Louis's college professors made sure that Louis was prepared to enter medical school.

_____ 7. Some of the medical school professors had high praise for Louis.

Name

Critical Thinking, Gray Level. © 1987 Steck-Vaughn Co.

Each generalization below states something that is not always true. Write a sentence of your own to show that the generalization is false, or **invalid**.

Example: Atomic energy is dangerous.

Atomic energy has been put to use to cure diseases.

1. Students who go out for athletics are not interested in schoolwork.

_____

_____

2. Exposure to sunlight causes skin cancer.

_____

_____

3. People who use surfboards like the feeling of danger.

_____

_____

4. Everyone should have a telephone-answering machine.

_____

_____

5. People who run for a political office only want power.

_____

_____

6. If you eat junk food, you are bound to get sick.

_____

_____

7. Television shows give you false ideas about the world.

_____

_____

Name _____

Read each paragraph. On the lines below it, write a true, or **valid**, generalization you can make from the facts given in the paragraph.

1. Imagine what would happen if all the glass around you should suddenly disappear! Insulated glass is used for windows, because it lets in light but keeps out hot and cold air. Glass is used in light bulbs, television tubes, mirrors, camera lenses, and eyeglasses. Even some cooking utensils and curtains are made of glass.

_____

_____

_____

2. Have you ever examined the rings in a tree stump? Each ring is the result of one year's growth. Therefore, counting the number of rings will tell you the approximate age of the tree. The width of the rings shows whether the tree grew a lot or just slightly during a year. If the tree was damaged or diseased during its growth, that might result in fuzzy or partial rings.

_____

_____

_____

3. Much of the land around the equator in Africa is densely forested wilderness. Tall trees spread their branches, shading the ground with heavy foliage. Near the ground, vines and creepers climb the trees and hang from limb to limb. The shady ground is covered with a thick growth of bushes with stems and branches so closely connected that it is difficult to clear a path without cutting the growth with each step.

_____

_____

_____

Name _____

Critical Thinking, Gray Level. © 1987 Steck-Vaughn Co.

A **criterion** is a rule or guideline for judging or evaluating something. (The plural form of **criterion** is **criteria**.)

1. Suppose that your criterion for a tool is that it must measure time. Study the pictures below. Make an **X** on the tool or tools that do not meet that criterion.

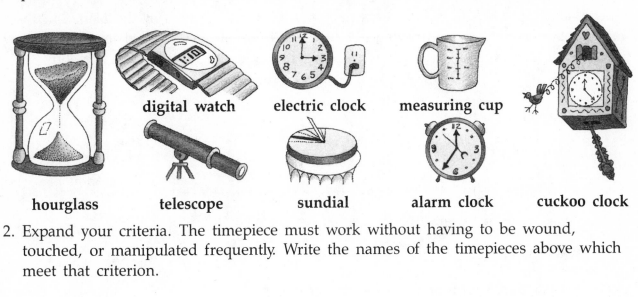

digital watch   **electric clock**   **measuring cup**

hourglass   **telescope**   **sundial**   **alarm clock**   **cuckoo clock**

2. Expand your criteria. The timepiece must work without having to be wound, touched, or manipulated frequently. Write the names of the timepieces above which meet that criterion.

_____

_____

_____

3. Change your criteria. The timepiece must make an obvious sound. Which timepieces above fill that criterion?

_____

_____

4. Imagine that you have been asked to design a wholly new kind of timepiece. You can make up your own criteria. What will they be?

_____

_____

_____

_____

Name _____

As you read, you often come across words that are unfamiliar to you. As a criterion for figuring out a word's meaning, you can use the context—or sentence—in which the word is used. As new details are provided in the sentence, your idea about the word's meaning can change.

Read sentence **1**. Use only the information in sentence 1 to fill in the blanks in the sentence below it. Next read sentence **2**. Use the information provided in sentence 2 to fill in the sentence below it. Continue in this manner for all the sentences on this page.

1. Betsy was given a **tessera**.

   A **tessera** could be a _____, a

   _____, or a _____.

   | scarf |
   | mosaic glass |
   | wooden block |

2. Betsy was given a **tessera** that had a hard surface.

   A **tessera** could be a _____ or a _____.

3. The **tessera** had a hard surface that reflected light.

   A **tessera** is a _____.

4. Did you see the **ouzel**?

   An **ouzel** could be a _____, a

   _____, or a _____.

   | lion |
   | garment |
   | bird |

5. Did you see the **ouzel** eating its meal?

   An **ouzel** could be a _____ or a _____.

6. Did you see the **ouzel** eating seeds and berries?

   An **ouzel** is a _____.

Name _____

Critical Thinking, Gray Level. © 1987 Steck-Vaughn Co.

Suppose that your class is having a Riddle-Search Contest. You must find riddles that follow different criteria.

Criterion 1: Find a riddle that **does not** rhyme.

Criterion 2: Find a riddle that **does** rhyme.

1. Write **Criterion 1** or **Criterion 2** above each riddle below.

_____ A box without hinges, key, or lid, Yet golden treasure inside is hid.	_____ I can go up the chimney down, But not down the chimney up.

— from *The Hobbit* by J.R.R. Tolkien

2. On the lines below, write your own riddle to follow Criterion 1.

_____

_____

_____

3. Now write your own riddle that follows Criterion 2.

_____

_____

_____

4. Develop your own criteria for the Riddle-Search Contest. For example, you might specify that all riddles must be on a certain subject, or that all riddles must be based on homophones (words that sound alike). Write your Riddle-Contest criteria below.

_____

_____

_____

Name _____

Writers often follow certain criteria as they compose stories and poems. Here are the criteria for the poetry form called **haiku**:

- A **haiku** has three lines.
- When spoken aloud, the first and third lines have five syllables.
- When spoken aloud, the second line has seven syllables.

A. Does the following poem meet the criteria for a haiku? To find out, make a mark over each syllable in the poem.

> An old silent pond . . .
> A frog jumps into the pond,
> splash! Silence again.
> —*Basho*

B. Complete the following sentence by first circling the correct word or word group in parentheses and then finishing the sentence in your own words.

The poem by Basho (**is**, **is not**) a haiku, because _____

_____

_____

C. Another kind of poem is called a **tanka**. Here are the criteria:

- A **tanka** has five lines.
- The first and third lines have five syllables each.
- The second, fourth, and fifth lines have seven syllables each.
- A **tanka**, like a **haiku**, usually tells about a scene from nature.

On the lines below, write your own tanka. Keep the criteria in mind.

_____

_____

_____

_____

_____

Name _____

Critical Thinking, Gray Level. © 1987 Steck-Vaughn Co.

When you read or listen, evaluate the accuracy of what the writer or speaker is saying. For example, listen or read to make sure there are no **contradictions**. In a contradiction, a person says one thing, and then later on says something that is just the opposite.

Read the following selections. Find and underline the sentences in each that contradict one another.

1. You can learn a lot by raising a young animal that you have found in the wild, such as a red squirrel or a raccoon. If you find a wild animal that is hurt or sick, call your local Humane Society. The people there will urge you to return the animal to its natural environment. When you raise a wild pet in your home, the Humane Society will gladly help you out.

2. In every state in the United States, it is a law that children must attend school until a certain age. Unless you attend school until that age, you or your parents could be taken to court. The law allows that "school" can mean being taught at home by your parents or going to a private school. In Mississippi, there is no law about attending school.

3. Most Americans respect George Washington, our first President, and have a special regard for his honesty. When Washington was only six years old, he admitted to his father that he had cut down a prized cherry tree. There is little doubt that Washington valued honesty and loyalty in government. The story about the cherry tree was made up by a man named Parson Weems, who sold 50,000 copies of his book about George Washington's life.

4. Children who run away from home often feel that they have very good reasons for doing so. Home may be a place where there is a lot of trouble and fighting, and it's best to stay away. Home is still the place where you can get the best help. Runaway children can get back home by calling one of the many "hotlines" for runaways.

Name

When you are reading or listening, check to make sure that the conclusion follows logically from the facts that are given. If the conclusion does that, then it is accurate.

Study the picture and words below. Then do the activities.

A. What is the speaker's conclusion? _____

_____

B. Why are the two young people in the audience doubtful about the conclusion?

_____

_____

C. Imagine that you are the speaker's speech writer. List three possible facts that the speaker could use to justify the conclusion "Vote for me!"

    1. _____

    2. _____

    3. _____

Name
_____

Critical Thinking, Gray Level. © 1987 Steck-Vaughn Co.

Good writers and speakers provide their audiences with specific details and vivid word pictures. Their words, phrases, and sentences give evidence that they have studied their subjects well and have thought about them thoroughly.

A. Read the following paragraphs. As you read, underline the words and phrases that make a coral reef glow in your "mind's eye."

Swim out over a coral reef, and you see coral shaped like rocks, stars, fingers, or fans. There is coral shaped like animal horns and antlers, even like trees and bushes. There is coral of all colors—tan, orange, yellow, purple, green, and pink.

A coral reef is an underwater range of stone hills. It forms in the shallow, warm oceans of the world. The warm temperature of the water and a good supply of sunlight are needed for the coral to grow. It is built up, bit by bit, over thousands of years by the remains of sea plants and animals. The largest coral reef in the world is the Great Barrier Reef off the coast of Australia. It is hundreds of feet wide and over one thousand miles long.

— from *The Coral Reef* by Gilda Berger

B. You may not be able to explore a coral reef as Gilda Berger did. But you **can** examine some part of **your** environment very carefully and write about it in detail. Choose something you see near you now—a book, a table, a window, a picture—and describe it precisely on the lines below.

_____

_____

_____

_____

_____

_____

Name _____

Sometimes, when you are reading or listening, you come upon a statement that makes you say to yourself, "That doesn't sound right! That doesn't fit in with what I already know."

Follow through with your feelings. You may be wrong, or you may be right. Maybe you have found some evidence that the writer or speaker was in error. Do some research and find out for sure.

Read the items below. Circle the ones that seem to have one or more obvious errors in them. Check the facts. Then rewrite the items you have circled to make them accurate.

1. Teenage girls are involved in more automobile accidents than are teenage boys.

2. The era of clipper ships was not one for cowardly sailors. The workers who handled these steamships were known for their courage and daring.

3. A **dowel** is a peg which is used to fasten two pieces of wood together.

4. Your science project will go well if you simply act on your own and ignore the advice of other people.

5. Most Spanish place names in the United States can be found in the northeastern part of the country.

Name _____

Critical Thinking, Gray Level. © 1987 Steck-Vaughn Co.

On many occasions, you are expected to provide **evidence** to prove that what you are saying is correct. Read about each situation described below. On the lines, write the kind of evidence you would expect each speaker to present.

1. One evening, a police officer stopped a driver who was moving along through traffic without using headlights. "I'm sorry, Officer," said the driver. "My headlights don't work. I just called the garage and was going there now to get the lights repaired."

   _____

   _____

2. The historical committee in a town asks that construction of a new housing project be stopped. "The site of the project," said the committee chief, "is an ancient Indian burial ground. It contains many valuable artifacts and should be preserved as a special forever-wild area."

   _____

   _____

3. The manufacturer of a new kind of glass claims that the product should be used for windows. A spokesperson for the company said, "The glass is unbreakable, conserves energy by keeping warm air from escaping, and lets in more light than other kinds of glass."

   _____

   _____

4. You announce after lunch that you found a valuable ring on the playground. "Hey, that's my ring," says one of your classmates. "I'm glad you found it. Please give it to me."

   _____

   _____

Name _____

In preparing a report, you are usually expected to use resource material to find facts about your subject and to check those facts. Read each subject below. Then look at the book titles in the picture at the bottom of the page. Write the titles of the books that you could consult for evidence.

1. a report on local moths and butterflies

_____

_____

2. a report on the rain forests of New Guinea

_____

_____

3. a report on nursing as a career

_____

_____

4. a report on English words from other languages

_____

_____

5. a report on the development of the interstate highway system

_____

_____

Name

Critical Thinking, Gray Level. © 1987 Steck-Vaughn Co.

Metaphors and **similes** are comparisons. A simile uses the word **like** or **as**. A metaphor does not use **like** or **as**.

A. Read each comparison below. Use the description above to decide whether the comparison is a simile or a metaphor. Then write **metaphor** or **simile** after the comparison.

1. The wind is a wolf that prowls at night. _____

2. The road is a ribbon of moonlight. _____

3. The leaves drop crisply, like ghostly footsteps. _____

4. He is as strong as a horse. _____

5. The stars lit our way like candles. _____

B.

1. Write two similes to describe the scene shown in the picture.

   a. _____

   b. _____

2. Now write two metaphors to describe the same scene. Try to develop different images than those you developed for similes.

   a. _____

   b. _____

Name _____

119

Imagine that you are the manager of a local radio station. A recent poll shows that fewer and fewer people are listening to your station. Listeners are turning the dial to other stations instead. Advertisers—who provide income for your station—are dropping their ads and placing them elsewhere.

A. With a classmate, brainstorm several ways in which you could get evidence that would help you decide what you should do to make the station popular again. List your ideas.

_____

_____

_____

_____

B. Now read your list. Check the two ideas that you think would bring in the most helpful information. On the lines below, tell how you would carry out those ideas.

1. _____

_____

_____

_____

2. _____

_____

_____

_____

C. Think ahead. Anticipate a problem you might run into as you collected your evidence. Describe the problem on the lines below.

_____

_____

Name _____

Critical Thinking, Gray Level. © 1987 Steck-Vaughn Co.

Values are standards of behavior that people think are important. People often have different values, and that might cause a conflict. The story below tells about a value conflict. After you have read the story, answer the questions that follow it.

Julie didn't want to baby-sit for her younger sister and brother, but she had promised her mother to do a good job. Julie knew the rules: only one hour of TV, lots of outdoor exercise, and a healthy lunch. She wondered whether Cora and Tommy would cooperate.

"Wow!" exclaimed Cora. "Since Mom's gone, we can watch TV all day."

"Great!" said Tommy. "I'll make us some lunch and we can eat it in here. We can share a sandwich and save our appetites for ice cream and cookies."

"Forget it!" said Julie. "You know Mom's rules. And I promised to follow them."

"Mom's not here," said Cora. "How's she going to know what we did?"

"Cora's right," said Tommy. "And Julie, I know **you** like TV and ice cream, too. Here is your chance to indulge yourself!"

"Please, Julie," whined Cora. "We'll be on our best behavior if you let us."

Julie thought to herself, "If I don't let Cora and Tommy have their way, they're going to make my day really tough. But if I give in, I'll be breaking my promise to Mom."

1. What do you think Julie should do? _____

_____

_____

2. How would that decision make her mother feel? _____

_____

_____

3. How would her decision make Cora and Tommy feel? _____

_____

Name _____

The values that many people hold today were set down long ago in sayings and proverbs.

A. Read each old saying. Use your own words to tell what the saying means.

1. He who hesitates is lost.

_____

_____

2. Better late than never.

_____

_____

3. Haste makes waste.

_____

_____

4. Slow and steady wins the race.

_____

_____

5. Don't put off until tomorrow what you can do today.

_____

_____

B. Read the sayings—and your versions of them—carefully. Do you find that any of

the values stated are in conflict? _____ Explain your answer on the lines below.

_____

_____

_____

Name _____

Critical Thinking, Gray Level. © 1987 Steck-Vaughn Co.

It often happens that a person's **own** values conflict with one another. Read about each person and situation. On the lines, tell **what** you think that person should do, and why you think he or she should do it.

1. Joel sets a high value on being kind to newcomers. He also sets a high value on playing fair and being a good sport.

    Kirk is a newcomer to school, and Joel, the captain of the kickball team, asks Kirk to join the team. During the very first game, Joel and his teammates notice that Kirk is a poor sport and often cheats. What should Joel, as captain, do?

    _____

    _____

    _____

2. Leon values honesty. He also values doing a good job on his schoolwork. He has been doing poorly in social studies, even though he has spent a lot of time studying.

    Tomorrow is the day of an important social studies test. Leon's friend Gary says, "I saw the teacher put the duplicated copies of the test in her desk drawer, and I'm going to take a copy at recess. Do you want me to get a copy for you, too?" What do you think Leon will do? Why?

    _____

    _____

    _____

3. Allison puts a high value on keeping her promises. She also puts a high value on friendship. Allison promised her little brother that she would take him to the park on Saturday. That morning Allison's friend Cindy calls and says, "Please come over. I feel so blue and need to talk to you alone." What do you think Allison should do? Why?

    _____

    _____

    _____

Name _____

Imagine that it is the year 3000. All Earth people must choose a new planet on which to live. Their choices are the planets Alpha, Beta, or Gamma. Read the descriptions of each planet.

Alpha People do not do physical labor. It is done by machines. Children are raised in nurseries. When they become adults, people work in computer centers or at television broadcasting facilities dedicated to entertainment.

Beta Children are raised at home. Everyone must either attend school or work. All Beta people live exactly the same kind of life. Special awards and prizes, however, are given to citizens who perform special acts for their planet.

Gamma Gamma is known as the old-fashioned planet. Each family has a farm and is expected to provide everything for itself, from food to clothing and housing. There are no schools on Gamma. Children learn their parents' tasks and carry on the work of the farm when they grow up.

A. None of these three planets may suit you exactly. But suppose that you must choose

one of them as your new home. Which planet would you choose? _____

Why? _____

_____

_____

B. Name three changes you would like to bring about on the planet you chose.

1. _____

2. _____

3. _____

Name _____

Critical Thinking, Gray Level. © 1987 Steck-Vaughn Co.

A writer builds a **mood**, or feeling, into a story in several ways. One of these ways is to appeal to values and emotions that many of us share. Read the story below. Then complete the activities.

Waiting

Hachi went to a Tokyo railroad station to see his master off to work as usual one day in 1925. At five o'clock, the faithful dog went to meet his master's homecoming train. But that night, his master did not appear and never would again, for he had died during the day.

How was the loyal little dog to know that? Never giving up hope, Hachi went to the railroad station every day for the next ten years and waited for the five o'clock train. When his master did not appear, the dog slunk sadly home again.

The story of the persistent dog spread throughout Japan, and the people came to love this special canine. When Hachi died, the Japanese government built a statue of the dog on the very spot where he had always waited. Tiny replicas of the statue were sent to all the schools in the nation.

1. In the story, find and underline the words or phrases that appeal to values of **affection**, **loyalty**, and **hope**.

2. Circle the phrase that sets a mood of despair or unhappiness.

3. Stories about dogs appeal to a great many people. On the lines below, list some reasons why this may be so.

_____

_____

4. Suppose that you are about to write a story or brief description of a dog. What

mood would you try to establish? _____

What words or phrases could you use to establish that mood? _____

_____

Name

Writers also establish story mood by carefully constructing descriptions of characters and by giving these characters dialogue that shows the character in action.

Read each paragraph below. On the line before each paragraph, write a word from the box that best describes the character's mood or personality.

curious	ashamed	worried	grateful	kindhearted	angry

_____ 1. Vern pounded his fist on the table as he yelled at his brother. "How many times have I told you not to touch my experiment? You've ruined it! Now I'll have to start all over again," said Vern.

_____ 2. Sadie hung her head. "How could I have been so careless? Now none of you can go to the play, because I forgot to get the tickets. I'm so sorry," she said.

_____ 3. Owen walked to the window again and looked out at the storm. "I still don't see anyone coming down the road. The storm is getting worse. I hope they can get home safely," he said.

_____ 4. Ellen noticed a young boy sitting alone at the edge of the playground. She went over to him and suggested, "Come and join us. We're going to play dodge ball. If that isn't your favorite, we could play another game later."

_____ 5. Jesse purposely chose a seat in the cafeteria beside the new student. Before he even put his tray down, Jesse asked eagerly, "I hear you went to school in South America. What was it like? Which sports did you play?"

_____ 6. "Yes, it's my book. Thank you for bringing it to me. I'm glad you noticed it on the counter, because it was a present and I'm still reading it," said Lois to the stranger who had stopped her as she was leaving the store.

Name _____

Critical Thinking, Gray Level. © 1987 Steck-Vaughn Co.

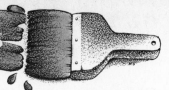

A Judging Accuracy
Making Decisions

This picture appeared in many newspapers all around the world in 1934. Study the picture for clues that will help you answer the questions below.

1. How can you tell that this is a birthday party?

_____

2. In what way do these five girls seem special?

_____

3. Suppose you are asked to find evidence to support your answer to question 2. What sources could you use?

_____

_____

_____

B Testing Generalizations

Study the following generalization. Then rewrite it to make it valid.

All children who are special get a lot of publicity and extra attention.

_____

_____

Name _____

127

C. Mood of a Story
Developing Criteria

Read the poem. Then complete the activities that follow it.

Mama Is a Sunrise

When she comes slip-footing through the door,
   she kindles us
   like lump coal lighted,
   and we wake up glowing.
She puts a spark even in Papa's eyes
and turns out all our darkness.

When she comes sweet-talking in the room,
   she warms us
   like grits and gravy,
   and we rise up shining.
Even at night-time Mama is a sunrise
that promises tomorrow and tomorrow.
      —Evelyn Tooley Hunt

1. Write a sentence that describes the mood of the poem.

_____

_____

2. On the lines below, develop two sets of criteria—one for the "perfect parent" and one for the "perfect child."

Perfect Parent   **Perfect Child**

_____   _____

_____   _____

_____   _____

Name _____

Critical Thinking, Gray Level. © 1987 Steck-Vaughn Co.

128